Big Design, Small Budget

Big Design, Small Budget

Create a Glamorous Home in Nine Thrifty Steps

BETSY HELMUTH

Photography by John Ha

Skyhorse Publishing

Skyhorse Publishing books may be purchased in bulk at special discounts for sales promotion, corporate gifts, fund-raising, or educational purposes. Special editions can also be created to specifications. For details, contact the Special Sales Department, Skyhorse Publishing, 307 West 36th Street, 11th Floor, New York, NY 10018 or info@skyhorsepublishing.com.

Skyhorse® and Skyhorse Publishing® are registered trademarks of Skyhorse Publishing, Inc.®, a Delaware corporation.

Visit our website at www.skyhorsepublishing.com.

10 9 8 7 6 5 4 3 2 1

Library of Congress Cataloging-in-Publication Data is available on file.

Cover design by Brian Peterson
Cover photo credit: John Ha

ISBN: 978-1-62914-549-5
Ebook ISBN: 978-1-62914-872-4

Printed in China

I am inspired daily by my husband's patience and my mother's love.
This book is for you, Jack Helmuth and Donna Head.
B.H.

Contents

Introduction

Before we become well acquainted in the following chapters, allow me to introduce myself. My name is Betsy Helmuth, and I own Affordable Interior Design in New York City. I have designed over 1,000 spaces, including a palatial NYC penthouse, a Vermont log cabin, a pied-à-terre in Argentina—heck, even a McDonald's in Brooklyn!

In this book, I am spilling my design secrets. I am giving away the gold. I want you to have a lovely home—without a huge budget, without the help of a personal designer, and without an illusive "eye for design." I want this to be the guide that helps you create a space you love to come home to.

A well-designed place is something everyone can achieve using principles that apply to any home. Let's take the pretension and mystery out of it. My design rules are easy and fun—if I do say so myself!

PORTRAIT OF THE ARTIST AS A YOUNG DESIGNER

This story of how I became an interior designer is one that I rarely share—and I almost never tell the *full* story. Not even my husband knew the whole of it until he read the draft of this book.

I started my design career as a painter. I made paintings for people's apartments. They commissioned pieces, and I would go to their spaces to measure and determine what their custom art should look like. Too often, I would walk into these fabulous apartments and be really let down. Their furniture would be too big, haphazard, illogically placed—and super expensive.

My clients would insist that a great piece of art would bring everything in their sad spaces together. They hoped something stretched on canvas would save the day. Fat chance. One day I let the cat out of the bag. I told one of my clients that his apartment was tragic. I told him that not even an original Van Gogh was going to give his space style. (I am known for my tact.) I offered to give him a sketch for a total redesign of his apartment and a sketch for a painting. He could decide which to move forward with, same charge either way.

He went with the redesign, and my life forever changed. I poured my heart and soul into that project. I had to prove to him (and to myself) that I could make his space fabulous. I binge-watched interior design shows, designed custom shelving, bought butcher's wax to create a faux-leather wall, sampled endless paint colors, supervised contractors, and made a couple of original paintings to boot.

He loved it. It looked amazing! On the very last day of work, I returned to the space with the carpenter to install the pièce de résistance: my custom shelves. I had my camera in hand. I couldn't wait to take pictures of my masterpiece. I had done it!

I approached the doorman, and he notified me that the tenant had denied access. Long story short: my client had lost his job, was moving out, and I was not getting paid. All those paint samples, wood chips, and cans of wax—I would be eating those along with my fee.

Williamsburg

Financial District

Park Slope

Vermont

Dumbo

I got burned, but beneath my anger and sadness, a spark had been ignited. I had found a passion for design. I had designed a place that turned out fabulously. But, obviously, I didn't know the first thing about the business of design. I knew I needed to know more.

The only mentors I knew to turn to were the designers I had watched on TV. I naively googled Thom Filicia from *Queer Eye for the Straight Guy* and called his firm. Two days later, I had an interview in his Soho offices. My painting portfolio won me an apprenticeship, and my design career began.

The first day I showed up with a bag lunch and a bit of panic. They sent me to a high-end store with a corporate card and instructions to buy juice glasses for a house in the Hamptons. Huh? The cheapest glass in the store was $40—for ONE GLASS! I was feverish. I came back with a few, and nobody flinched at the receipt. We were designing for celebrities, and the world was our oyster.

I would regularly order a lamp or throw pillow that cost more than my Manhattan rent. Internally, I was aghast. Filling out the purchase orders, my brain would be spinning: Didn't I see a lamp like that at Crate and Barrel? Can't I get a pillow that same color at West Elm for one-tenth of the price?

After absorbing Thom's impeccable sense of style and learning some business savvy, I ventured out on my own. In 2005, I started Affordable Interior Design, determined to prove that elegant living need not be exclusively for the elite. I knew the principles I learned could be implemented for a fraction of the high-end price.

MY RULES

For the first time, I am outlining my principles. I have tested them over the past nine years and 1,000+ designs. These are the rules I use every day.

Not only am I a seasoned designer, I also fancy myself a psychic. I can hear you asking, "Why do I have to follow rules? I bet Thom doesn't refer to a mental manual when designing. He has a mystical way of picking things out."

I hear you. While I am sure somewhere in the back of his head he refers to rules, outwardly he is effortlessly able to make things go together. Thousands of hours of practice make perfect. Plus, it is also a lot easier to make things work when you have a bottomless budget.

Experts, like Thom Filicia, and millionaires, like his private clients, do not have to follow rules. Example: Jennifer Lopez calls Thom (in my mind's eye, I imagine she does regularly). She found a fabulous mirror in Paris that is huge and disproportionately large for her dressing area. It goes against the rules of scale. Is Thom going to tell her he can't make it work because it breaks design rules? Uh, no. You don't tell J. Lo no. Marc Anthony learned that lesson the hard way.

Instead, Thom will make that mirror work by shelling out big bucks for custom solutions. He will design a bespoke settee to place in front of it, create lighting effects to dwarf it, and install built-in shelving around it. Voila! If you are an expert or a millionaire, no need to follow my rules.

If you don't fall into these two categories, get out a highlighter. When designing on a budget, we need guidelines to get it right. No second-guessing. No regrets. No custom.*

The tips in the following chapters guarantee a great look without a celebrity designer or a magical eye for design. This is the way that I work. This is *Big Design, Small Budget.*

"BUT, BETSY, DO YOU EVER BREAK YOUR OWN RULES?"

Readers, I never break my rules—unless I have to. Hidden in these pages, you may see a few pics that contradict my guidelines. My clients are on a tight budget, and sometimes we have to reuse things that are not ideal. Sometimes my clients are adamant about buying one of my no-nos, like a solid rug, a print of a painting, or a leather sectional. The customer is king. So if you spy an atrocity in the pages that follow, remember, I was forced to commit it.

---

*At Affordable Interior Design, we never use the dreaded "C" word—custom. Custom is too expensive and takes too long for my clients. We need to work with what we can find retail.

CHAPTER 1:
THE BOTTOM LINE

The most important question that I ask my clients is: "What is your budget?" 99% of the time I get a blank stare as they reply, "I don't know. You tell me how much I should spend." Unacceptable. Getting a bottom line is vital. It determines how many pieces we will reuse, how many we can buy, where we will shop, if we will be dumpster diving.

I get a firm answer to my question nearly every time when I cut to the chase and ask, "What is the most you would want to spend?" Take a moment and ask yourself, what number makes you start to sweat? Is it $2,000? $5,000? $15,000? That number, dear readers, is your budget.

KEEPING IT REAL: COMMITMENT

Committing to a home is just like committing to a partner. Whether you rent or own, whether you have a steady boyfriend/girlfriend or a husband/wife, you gotta love the one you're with.

So many times I have a client who picks their place apart: It's too small. It's not my ideal neighborhood. I wish the ceilings were higher. I wish he'd put the seat down.

You chose your space (and your significant other) for a reason. There was something you loved (the price, the school district, his hairline) that made you say yes. Remember those reasons and embrace its/his attributes rather than focusing on the flaws. When you treat your place with love, investing time and money into making it yours, you will reap rewards—at home and in your relationship.

BUDGET QUIZ

When working with my clients, I don't care how much money they make or how much they have saved. What I care about is how much they want to invest in this space at this stage of their lives.

Let me show you what I mean. I'm going to make all this money talk a little more palatable with a Budget Quiz. Get a pen, pour yourself an adult beverage (finances should be fun!), and we will determine how much you should spend.

I.   **Do you rent or own?**

   a.   Rent. You're going to be in the space one to three years. You want to be content, but there is no guarantee that the pieces you buy will be able to move with you.

   b.   Long-Term Rent. You are going to be in the space more than three years. You are ready to settle in and start feeling at home.

   c.   Own but on the Fence. You may stay one to two years more. You may rent it out in the near future. Heck, you may even put it on the market. Just because you have took a mortgage on it doesn't mean you are still committed. The changes you make will help the place "show" better for future renters/buyers. Invest a bit but don't break the bank.

   d.   Own and Sticking with It. Settle in. Make some of your design dreams come true. Do it right so you won't have to do it again for a while.

2. How many new pieces do you need?
   a. A ton. You are starting from scratch.
   b. A lot. You are ready for an overhaul.
   c. Some. You're attached (financially or emotionally) to some pieces and ready to replace others.
   d. None. You'll work with what you have.

3. Do you live with kids?
   a. Yes, and they pretty much have the run of the place. Juice box mishaps, crayon marks on the couch, and stickers on the walls are realities at your house.
   b. Yes, but you lay down the law. There is no eating in the living room, the kids put their toys away dutifully, and they were born with an innate sense of self-control. Congrats, by the way.
   c. No, but you plan on having some in the next one to three years and/or you behave like a grown child. Spills will happen soon (or are happening). Spit up will happen soon (or is happening).
   d. No way or the kids are out of the house. Kids are not in the picture or they have their own homes to worry about.

4. Do you have pets?
   a. Yes, and you deal with accidents, chewing, and clawing regularly.
   b. Yes, but they are very well behaved. There is the occasional hairball; other than that, they are angels.
   c. No, not now. But maybe in the future.
   d. No, not happening—ever.

5. Do you plan on entertaining?
   a. Yes, between poker nights, play dates, book clubs, and out-of-town guests, your front door ought to be a revolving one. You need items that can withstand stains, provide plenty of seating, and leave money leftover to stock your home bar!

b. Yes, you have friends over once a month or so. Stain-resistant would be nice, and six dining chairs are a must.

c. No, on the rare occasion that someone stops by, you will make it work with what you have and/or inflate an air mattress.

d. No, your home is your hermitic sanctuary.

6. **What is the reaction you want your friends to have when they come over?**

a. "Wow! Elegant! I promise I won't break anything." To get a magazine-ready look, you must be prepared to pay the piper.

b. "Nice! I want to live here." Spend a little more to get a refined look.

c. "So much better. So comfortable." You'll need a few throw pillows and great seating, but you don't have to go nuts.

d. "Did you do something different with your living room?" Subtle touches/moves will make a big difference to you—even if no one else notices.

7. **Where do you shop for clothes?**

a. High-End Retail. You are accustomed to nice textures and materials. You won't be happy with anything less.

b. Mix and Match. You prefer high-end stores but mainly buy their sale items. Mostly you shop at mid-range retailers.

c. Department Stores. You take a practical approach to apparel shopping.

d. Call Me "Secondhand Roy/Rose." You are creative, love scouring clearance racks, and are used to thinking outside the big box stores. You will make things work!

Now let's add your response totals:

1. a. 1, b. 3, c. 2, d. 4
2. a. 4, b. 3, c. 2, d. 1
3. a. 1, b. 3, c. 2, d. 4
4. a. 1, b. 2, c. 3, d. 4
5. a. 2, b. 1, c. 3, d. 4
6. a. 4, b. 3, c. 2, d. 1
7. a. 4, b. 3, c. 2, d. 1

7-13 POINTS

Be thrifty. You are going to have to shop low-end retailers like Target, Overstock.com, and Ikea. I see garage and thrift store sale-ing, Craigslist surfing, and coupon clipping in your future. To avoid a look that reveals the corners you cut, don't buy a lot of items at any one place. Design with a mix of stores in mind.

14-19 POINTS

Get a combination of good quality and good-enough pieces (see Chapter 3 for guidance). In each room, make an expensive splash with a couple of large items of quality. Fill in with affordable choices. Then ice the cake with discount accents.

20-28 POINTS

Let's have some fun! You have money burning a hole in your pocket. Strategize so you don't buy every cool thing in sight. Find a couple of inspiration images on design sites or in this book, and make those dreams come true in a focused way. Look for pieces that will last, sprinkle in a few things that you love, and work on your will so those lovely legacy places will have a home for decades to come.

THE BEST DEALS
I'M FLOORED

Before I pay full price for larger items, I ask a salesperson if there is a floor model available. Sometimes there is one in the showroom or in the back for a deep discount. Couldn't hurt to ask! Being open to floor models has saved my customers a bundle. Some look like they just popped out of the box. Some have been handled, scratched, or jumped on (probably by me or my clients). However, perhaps you have naughty kids and/or pets, and a scuff here or there won't faze you.

I LOVE SPAM

I sign up to get email blasts from all my favorite retailers. I created a separate email box for my vendor spam to keep it separate from my day-to-day affairs. Once you do, you will be among the first to know about their newest lines, features, and closeouts. The early bird gets the best sale items.

LET'S BE FRIENDS

Befriend stores on social media sites like Facebook, Twitter, Instagram, and Pinterest. Their posts will give you sneak peeks at promotions. Additionally, stores often feature promo/coupon codes that are exclusive to their followers.

CONSIDER THIS: A WORD OF WARNING

When creating a budget for a wedding or event, planners recommend you allocate a percentage of your budget for incidentals that may pop up. Interior design is no different. Between shipping, taxes, and assembly costs, small fees really add up. I recommend setting aside 15-20% of your budget for these items.

Keep in mind that the prices you find at online-only retailers (like Overstock.com, Homedecorators.com, Allmodern.com, etc.) are often very low because the onus is on you to put these pieces together. Ikea's prices are astoundingly low. However, their items involve complicated assembly with lots of itty-bitty hardware. A simple-looking dresser takes hours for even a professional to put together.

Speaking of professionals, you need to ensure that the person putting your furniture together is an expert. Pieces are only as durable as the quality of their assembly. Unless you are super-handy and strong, hire someone.

Suddenly these budget items don't seem as affordable, right? Exactly. That's why I rarely purchase complicated items from assemble-it–yourself stores. By the time I pay my handyman for his hours of work, I could have spent the same amount on a comparable piece from a higher-end retailer. In other words, make sure the budget item is worth the hassle.

SHOW ME THE PROMO
(Being from Missouri, I couldn't help myself...)

Before buying, I go to the stores to feel, jump on, and check out their wares. Then, instead of buying on the spot, I go home to purchase the items online where I can use a promo code (some stores call it a coupon code) for a discount. Most places make you hunt for these secret codes. Just type the name of the store and "promo code" or "coupon code" into your Internet browser's search to find a list of possible codes.

If the first code you find doesn't yield a discount, don't get discouraged. I often have to try a few before finding one that applies to my purchase.

MAGIC MONTHS

In general, furniture stores (and apparel ones, too) liquidate their inventory in January and July every year. I call these the "Magic Months" and urge my clients to start their redesign a couple of weeks prior. That way they can preview the items, and then jump the minute the pieces go on sale. During these months, the clearance items don't last very long. Be prepared to buy to get the best bang for your buck.

This book has already paid for itself, and it's only Chapter 1! You're welcome.

CHAPTER 2:
FURNISHING FYI

Time to fill in your newfound layouts with some specific furnishings. My descriptions below will serve as your trusty guide when surfing the net or winding through furniture showrooms. I'll let you in on how much to spend, what to look for, and where to put your pieces. Aren't you glad you've got a pro by your side?

GOLD NUGGETS

Before I talk about the specific pieces individually, I want to start you off with four essential rules of thumb. Do not start your shopping until you have put a big ol' circle around these gold nuggets. They are the most important tips in the whole dang book:

1. **Say No to Sets.** Furniture sets are a designer's nightmare. Buying a living room set, complete with coordinating coffee table, side tables, and console, is a sure-fire way to show that you have no style. Instead, you surrendered to the furniture gods, taking the easy and visually boring way out.

   As designers, we look for things that GO together but never CAME together. We want the pieces to coordinate effortlessly, but we don't want them to look the same. The magic in good design is contrast.

   Never ever buy a set or even too many pieces from the same store. You don't want your home looking like a catalog. You want it to be a well-curated space of disparate pieces.

2. **The Mix.** The fastest way to get a high-end look on a small budget is to mix many different materials in the same visual moment. For instance, if I have a wood nightstand, I will never put a wood lamp atop it. I will use a glass, metal, ceramic, or acrylic one. I want to mix in a new material/texture. I'm going to choose a mercury glass lamp for this scenario.

   Atop the nightstand, I want to put a picture frame. I want to be sure it is made of a new material. Therefore, I am not going to use a wood picture frame or a glass one. Instead, I

am going to use a black one. Someone reading this book is going to write me an email. Someone is going to point out that under that black paint it is wood. Yes, someone, you are right. However, painted wood does not count as a wood material. If I can't see a wood grain through the paint, it does not count as a wood element. Instead, it counts as a black element.

Therefore, if I want to put a tray on the lower shelf of the nightstand, I can't use a black tray. Black has already been done, as has wood and glass. I need to choose a new color/ texture, like acrylic, ceramic, metal, etc. In this case, I will pick a white one.

If you have not already deduced it, what I am going for is contrast. To get a complex and designerly look, each moment throughout your space should contain a mix of textures and elements.

3. **Wood Agreement.**★ When selecting wood furniture for your space, be sure that you stick with all dark woods (chocolate, rubber wood, espresso), all medium tone woods (walnut, maple, acacia), or all light woods (beech, pine, birch). The tones don't have to be an exact match, just in the same family. When I squint, I want to see a similar shade.

When choosing your furniture's wood family, no need to coordinate with the wood floors or architecture of the space.

DARK WOODS

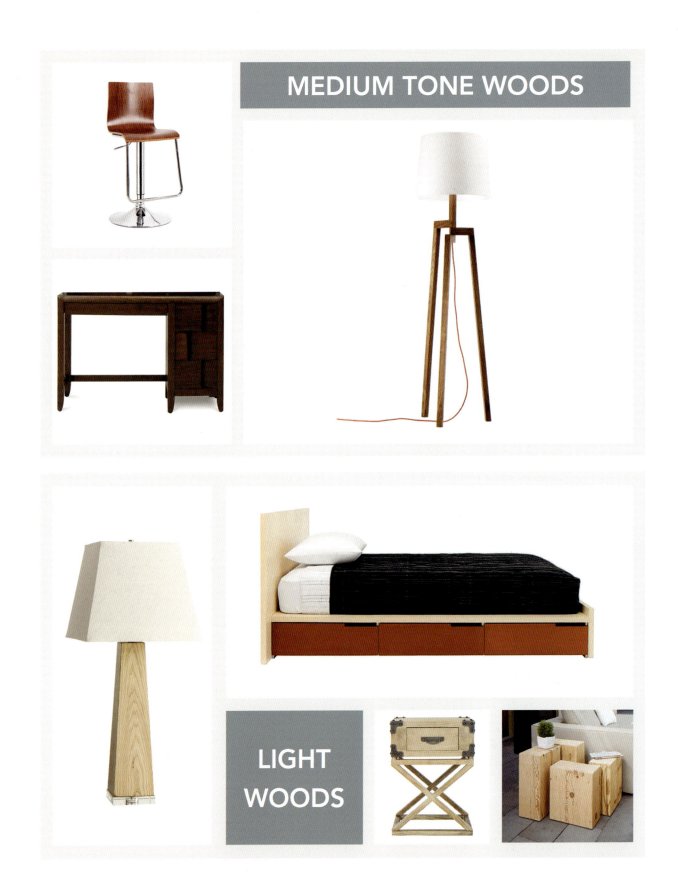

MEDIUM TONE WOODS

LIGHT WOODS

4. **Metal Agreement.** * Almost the exact same deal with your metals. You want to stick to all cool metals (nickel, silver, pewter), all warm metals (brass, gold, copper), or all dark metals (antique bronze, natural steel, wrought iron).

However, in this case, you pay attention to the metals that are featured in the architecture of your space (i.e., follow the lead of the hinges and knobs). In the very sad case that you have those '80s, fake-brass architectural details (like I do in my current rental), change them with a quickness or ignore them and choose a different metal finish for your furnishings.

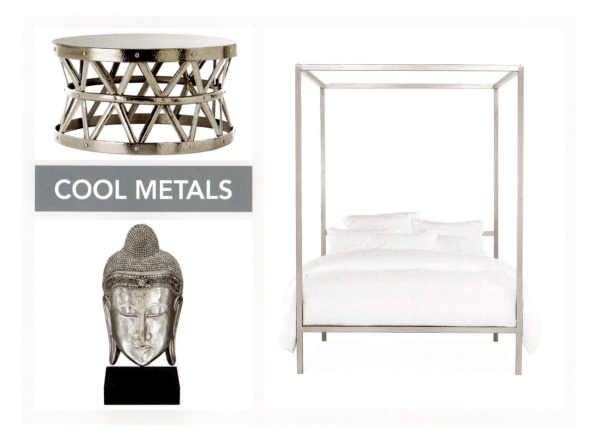

COOL METALS

---

*In magazines or froufrou design books, you will see the pros use a variety of wood tones and metal finishes within one room. Good for them. To do this, you have to have that elusive "eye for design." If you are not an expert, stick to the above agreements to get a cohesive look easily.

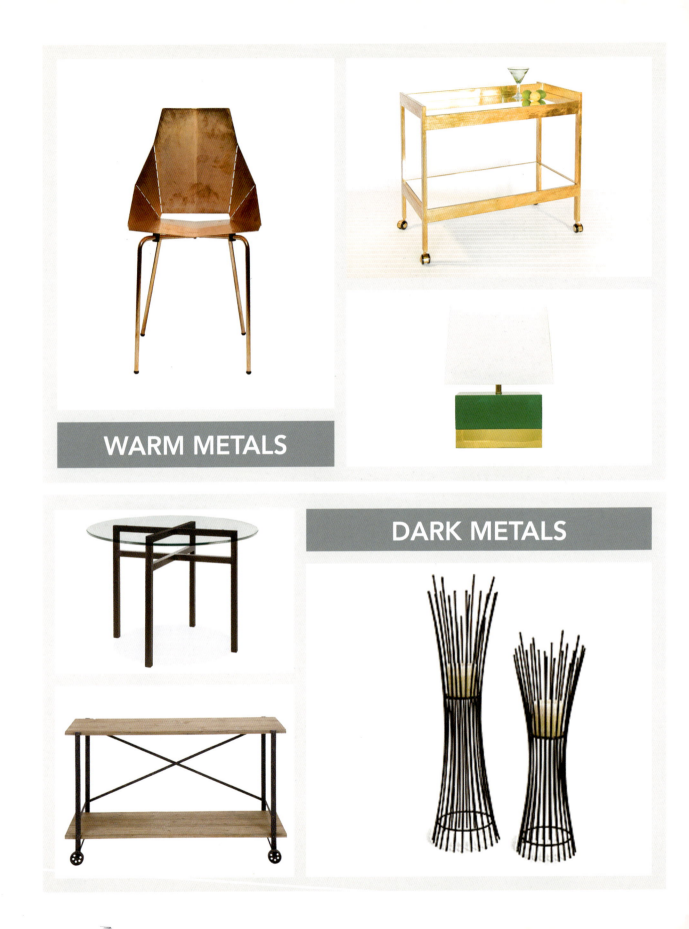

WARM METALS

DARK METALS

DEFINITIONS

Splurge

Go outside your financial comfort zone for these pieces. Spending a little more will go a long way in making your home look and feel fabulous.

Go the Distance

Shop low- and high-end to find the piece that works best for you. In this category, you will find items of good quality at many different price points.

Save

Great options are available at low price points.

PIECES/PRICES/PLACEMENT
SOFAS/SECTIONALS (Go the Distance)

Second to your bed, this is the piece you will be spending most of your time on. Finding a sofa/sectional that your entire family agrees is comfy is like searching for the Holy Grail. Leave no store unturned when looking for this most important of pieces. (Confession: My husband and I sat on every sofa in NYC before finding one both our butts could agree on—at Ikea of all places!)

Look For:

- Fabric upholstery. Leather is too expensive, doesn't breathe well (TMI alert: You get sweaty after sitting on it for a length of time), and serves as a slip and slide for your throw pillows/blankets.
- A mid-tone color. Anything too light, like white or cream, will show every stain. Anything too dark, like chocolate or black, will show every piece of lint. You are more likely to tire of a bold colored upholstery and it is less likely to go with the rest of your accessories. Pick a neutral fabric that has a very dull name. I love names like Taupe, Putty, Stone, and Beige. Mid-tone boring is the magic combo.

Positioning Pointers:

- Typically, this is the largest furniture piece in the room. As such, try it first on the longest wall where it will feel most grounded.
- Be sure that you can see the room's main point of access when seated on the sofa/sectional. Having your back to the entrance is the equivalent of being in the naughty corner, leaving you out of the loop from the room's goings-on.
- For the best first impression, I prefer the sofa on the wall kitty-corner from the main point of access. When guests walk in, they immediately see the most visually appealing moment in the room: the sofa with its plush pillows, surrounding art, anchored rug, and accessorized coffee table.

SIDE CHAIRS (Go the Distance)

Have some fun with your side chairs. Take a risk by choosing a pop of color, fun pattern, or new texture. Unlike the sofa, typically you don't sit in these for hours on end. This is the place to go for cool over comfort.

Sofa

Look for:

- **Cool shapes.** For a grand look, choose a high wingback. In a small space, pick rounded armchairs with no edges to bump into. If you want something that's barely there, go for an armless slipper chair. If you have an open space, a chaise longue (a.k.a. a chair with an attached ottoman) adds drama.
- **Opposing ottoman.** If you are really going to read or snuggle up in said chair, you need an ottoman. Get one in a contrasting fabric. Just be sure that the ottoman isn't wider than its chair.
- **Online deals.** Do a general Internet search for the color or style of chair you are looking for. There are tons of small shops that have funky options in a rainbow of hues and prints.

Side Chair

Positioning Pointers:

- Create an optimum conversation area by placing your side chairs parallel to the sofa.
- I often turn side chairs on the diagonal. The diagonal is the longest line in any room. Putting these on an angle encourages the eye to look in a new and space-expanding way.

ACCENT TABLES (Save)

You/your guest needs a place to put a drink, book, or a remote. Be they side, coffee, sofa, or console, these tables can be found for a steal.

Look for:

- **Table alternatives.** Your room doesn't have to be littered with tables. I like to get creative, using unexpected pieces like ceramic garden stools, trunks, upholstered ottomans with trays, a stack of books, or nesting tables.
- **Different materials.** Your coffee table, end table, sofa table, and console table should be a mix of different materials. We are avoiding the dreaded look of a set, remember?
- **Different shapes.** If I have a rectangular console table, I'll go for an oval coffee table. If I have a rectangular coffee table, I'll choose a round side table. You not only want an array of materials, you also want an assortment of shapes in your space.
- **Room to move.** Inside a sectional, I like to use a round coffee table as rectangular or square ones often fit tightly like a puzzle piece and restrict legroom.

Positioning Pointers:

- Every seat in your room (i.e., sofa, side chair, chaise, bench) needs a surface. Do this test: pour yourself a cocktail and sit in each seat. If you can't stretch your arm and rest the glass on a surface, that area needs an accent table.
- Nesting tables can liberate a room's layout. Rather than having tables littered around, these stack. Bring the smaller ones out when someone's in the seats and tuck them away when they're not needed.
- I don't like the overly symmetrical look of an end table on each side of a sofa. Instead, I prefer a floor lamp on one side and an end table on the other.

MEDIA STORAGE/ENTERTAINMENT CENTERS (Splurge)

Let's face it: the focal point in most living rooms is the television—in mine, too. No judgment. Since we are likely staring at the TV and the furniture it is in/on/above, I want that media storage to look nice.

Look for:

- **Cord concealment.** A media console or center must conceal the mess of cords behind it. I cringe when I see a glass or open-backed shelving media stand. I am very adamant about this one. Imagine me yelling a la Joan Crawford, "NO MORE VISIBLE CORDS— or wire hangers!"
- **Low sight lines.** If you choose to mount your TV above its stand, don't go too high. TVs are supposed to be viewed at eye level when you are seated on your sofa. When mounted too high (or, gosh forbid, above a fireplace), it can feel like you are seated in the front row of a movie theatre, cricking your neck to view the image above you.
- **Storage.** Besides just a cable box, media players, and gaming consoles, we typically have extra remotes, controllers, and DVDs that we need to store. Get a piece that can accommodate these items as well.
- **A Hallelujah Moment.** Let's just say you need a lot of storage. Let's just say your husband is a hoarder—like mine. He owns over 1,300 DVDs. Rather than having these in a collection of bookcases sprinkled around the room, I got a big ol' media center. Big. Hallelujah. This piece has saved our marriage. When clients have a lot of things, be they books, toys, just crap they can't part with, I recommend a media center. In order to not have the media center look like the big, DVD-stuffed elephant in the room, our unit has both open and closed storage. Most of the media is behind closed doors. Then we have featured the more interesting volumes as well as photos in frames and

Accent Tables

special mementos on the open shelves. Thus, the unit is more visually appealing and looks less like a storage locker.

Positioning Pointers:

- The unit should be placed so that the television is centered on the sofa or the primary seat from which it is watched.
- Double-check your room's balance. If you have a large sectional or sofa on one wall, you'll need more than just a small TV stand opposite it. Flank the TV stand with bookcases or go for an entertainment center.
- On the flip side, if you have a big entertainment center, you need more than a wilting loveseat on the wall opposing it. Bulk the seating area up with a chunky side table or a sizeable piece of art above the settee.

SHELVING/BOOKCASES (Save)

Your étagère is going to be mostly concealed behind books, picture frames, and baskets. We are looking for sturdy—not flashy.

Look for:

- **Depth.** It's a pet peeve of mine when things stick over the front of a bookcase. If you have wide books or want to store your board games on shelves, be sure you pick a deeper than normal bookcase.
- **Sides.** Having sides on your bookcase means that you can store more books within the piece. If your piece has open shelves with exposed ends, you are going to need bookends or you will need to lay books horizontally to prevent them from falling, which accommodates fewer tomes and tchotchkes.
- **Adjustable shelves.** Some books are tall. Some books are small. Maximize the amount you can store with adjustable shelves that leave 2-4" between the top of the books and the bottom of the next shelf.
- **Fewer pieces.** Unless they are built in, more than two tall bookcases in one room can start to feel oppressive. If you have more stuff than two cases can hold, consider a Hallelujah Moment (see above) or getting wider than normal bookcases (30" wide or greater).

Bookcase

Positioning Pointers:

- A space feels more welcoming when your eye steps up with the furniture as you enter. Therefore, place smaller pieces near the entry and taller pieces, like bookcases, toward the farther ends of the room.
- A bookcase with cubbies rather than shelves makes a perfect sofa table when laid on its side.
- Create the look of a media center without committing to one large piece by placing a bookcase on either side of a TV stand.

DINING TABLES
(Go the Distance)

Your dining table needs to be able to adapt like no other piece in your home. From eating to crafts to homework to game night, it's where activities go down. This piece takes a beating but still needs to look nice.

Look for:

- **Something unexpected.** Since a dining table takes up a lot of real estate in a space, it can be fun to choose one that looks unique. Instead of a conventional choice, make yours a conversation piece by picking one in an unexpected material like metal, reclaimed wood, or anything painted a bold color.
- **Extension capabilities.** Just because you host the holidays doesn't mean you need a table to seat 10 day-to-day. A table with extension allows for options. It also gives you versatility should you move to a bigger/smaller space and need to change your table's size.

CONSIDER THIS: THE SPACE BETWEEN

Ensure you have a great flow by allotting the proper amount of room around your furniture pieces. Here are the industry standards:

- 30-36" for a walkway, 36-48" in areas of high-traffic or for an airy feel
- 14-18" between the sofa and coffee table
- 48-100" between the sofa and side chairs
- 2-4" between the sofa and end table or bed and nightstands
- 2-4" between the wall and piece against it (furniture should never touch the wall)
- 24-36" behind desk and dining chairs so they can push out with ease
- Allocate 24-30" for each dining chair and barstool so each person has enough elbow room.
- Calculate your correct TV size by measuring from the center of the sofa to the TV wall in inches and dividing that number by two. That number is the best TV size for the space.

- **Anything but glass.** Boy, do I hate glass tables. They may be easy to clean but you will be cleaning them constantly. They show every fingerprint, elbow mark, everything! Unless you are a Windex stockholder, no thanks.
- **Height, in certain circumstances only.** High top or pub tables are perfect in very small spaces. Their surface area can be smaller than a standard table and the stools tuck rather than splaying out like chairs. They aren't ideal for foodies who need room to accommodate lots of platters. They also don't work well for accommodating dinner parties as generally they sit four people max.

Dining Table

Positioning Pointers:

- The shape of your dining table is determined by the size of the space you have. If the walls and walkways create a square space for your dining area, you should get a circular or square table. If you have a rectangular space (80% of my clients do), you should buy a rectangular or oval table.
- Make sure the table is not the first surface you encounter when entering your home or it is sure to downgrade from dining area to dumping ground for purses, keys, and mail.

DINING SEATING (Go the Distance)

Dining chairs/stools need to be easy to clean and comfortable. Spend what it takes to fulfill both criteria.

Look for:

- **Comfort.** Let's keep it real: If my dining chairs aren't comfy, I am going to sit on the sofa to eat dinner, and that's not ideal. Plus, comfortable dining chairs can be used as extra living room seating when hosting larger parties.
- **No fabric.** Fabric gets stained and can be hard to clean—even the performance fabrics. Tie-on seat cushions are passé. When going for upholstered, I choose leather, which is both comfortable and easy to wipe off.
- **Contrast.** When I look at the dining area and squint, I don't want to see a big blob of brown. The chairs should be a different color and/or texture than the table.

Dining Seating

- **Avoid the motley crew.** Sometimes clients ask for an eclectic look with mismatched chairs. You need that "designer eye" to pull this off without it looking like you went dumpster diving. Instead, get matching chairs on the sides and select a different style for the head/foot chairs. Or use a bench on one side and chairs on the other.

Positioning Pointers:

- Because we want our dining area conveniently located near the kitchen, it often winds up beside a breakfast bar or island. If that bar or island has an overhanging countertop, it needs stools. Of course, the dining table also needs seating. So many seats back-to-back = conundrum! I make it better by making one set of seats backless. If the dining chairs have backs, I use saddle-style barstools without them. If I have a backless bench at the dining table, I use stools with backs at the counter.
- You need six to eight chairs on special occasions, but day-to-day it's more than your table should accommodate. Instead, use one of the extras as a desk chair, one as a vanity seat, and/or one in the entry for taking off shoes.

BUFFETS/CREDENZAS (Splurge)

Buffets (a.k.a. credenzas) are great areas to gain extra storage. They are also versatile. In one space, the piece is a buffet. In another space, it is a bar or an entry console or a TV stand. Spend a little money knowing that your buffet is a jack-of-many-trades and can provide a different function should you move to a different home.

Look for:

- **Closed storage.** Since a buffet is a low piece, the inside is not meant for display. Instead, buy something with doors that you can pack full with extra platters and bottles of wine.
- **A new material.** I don't want it looking like you bought a dining set. Pick a buffet that is a visibly different tone/texture than your dining table.
- **A tray.** A tray on a buffet transforms it into a bar when holding martini glasses and a shaker. When filled with mail and keys, the buffet is now an entry console. When showcasing canapés, the buffet is a serving surface. A tray, in a contrasting material to the buffet, of course, is a perfect way to transition your piece from one purpose to another.

Positioning Pointers:

- When used in a dining area, be sure you have enough room to fully open the buffet's doors/drawers without hitting the chairs.
- When used in an entryway, be sure that the deep credenza allows enough room for a walkway.
- When used as a TV stand, be sure that the sofa is of standard height and the room deep enough so that the TV does not feel freakishly high when placed atop it.

DESKS/DESK CHAIRS (Go the Distance)

If/when I have my own furniture line, I will start by designing desks. Almost all of my clients request a desk, and the current retail selection of decent work surfaces is slim.

Look for:

- **Storage.** I don't care if you need storage or not. Every desk I recommend to my clients has storage underneath. We all need a place to put a pair of scissors. But the real reason your desk needs storage is that the drawers/shelves conceal those pesky cords. The cords from the desk lamp or chargers can all fall behind the trusty column of drawers/doors.
- **Anything but glass and open shelving.** Again, Mama don't wanna see your fingerprints or your cords! Get something opaque with closed storage.
- **A comfy seat.** If you spend a lot of time at your desk, you may want to sit on something ergonomic. Nearly all of those chairs look hideous. I surrender. Get the hideous yet super comfortable chair. Take the money you would have spent on a chiropractor and invest in a super chic desk that steals focus.
- **No wheels.** Unless your desk is on tile or a very low-pile rug (NO MORE PLASTIC FLOOR MATS!), you should not have wheels on your chair. Wheels will eat up your wood flooring, leaving unsightly gouges.

Positioning Pointers:

- Place it far from the entryway to avoid the dumping ground issue outlined in the dining area section.
- Another reason to keep it away from the entry is to avoid seeing it. Most of our desks are messy and functional rather than pristine and perfect. Don't nobody want to see

Desk

your printer or paperwork. Find an out-of-the-way corner in which to tuck it rather than making it the room's focal point.

- What's the word for an anti-aphrodisiac? For the purposes of this book, it will be "desk." Desks, with their technological energy, flashing lights, and stress-inducing projects, are far from sexy or restful. Keep them out of your bedroom.

RUGS (Save)

Rugs are one of the biggest elements in any space. They visually separate rooms into zones, create sensual experiences for our tootsies, and their patterns can serve as artistic statements for our floors. Tons of great textures and patterns can be found for a steal, so why spend a lot?

Look for:

- **A mid-tone color.** As with sofas, white or cream rugs show every stain. Black, navy, and dark brown show every dust bunny and sock fuzz ball.
- **A pattern.** Between walking, spills, and hairballs, rugs get a lot of wear. A patterned rug will camouflage these stains, giving it longevity.
- **Size.** The bigger the rug, the bigger the zone you are creating will look. In a living room, get a rug that is large enough to fit at least partially under all the pieces of seating (i.e., sofa, side chairs, chaise, and so on). In a dining room, it needs to be big enough so when you pull out your chair, you are still fully on the rug.
- **The right fiber.** Wool rugs are the standard. However, if you spend a lot of time on your rug playing with your kids/pets/PlayStation, wool rugs (like their sweater counterparts) can be itchy. Additionally, wool rugs usually shed for as long as three months. If you aren't a fan of vacuuming and want to play in comfort, opt for a synthetic texture like a polyester, acrylic, or nylon instead.
- **The right pile.** Anything under .25" in pile height is a flat-style rug that will likely move and wrinkle but be easy to clean. Anything between .25-.75" is a normal pile height and will be plush without being furry. Anything over .75" is entering shag territory. Mama don't do shag (see page 151 for a full explanation.) No matter your pile height, use a pad with every rug in your home to prevent shifting, buffer sound, and add cushioning.

Positioning Pointers:

- If you are going to have more than one rug in a room, you need to be sure that they are placed at least two feet apart. Without ample room between them, they com-

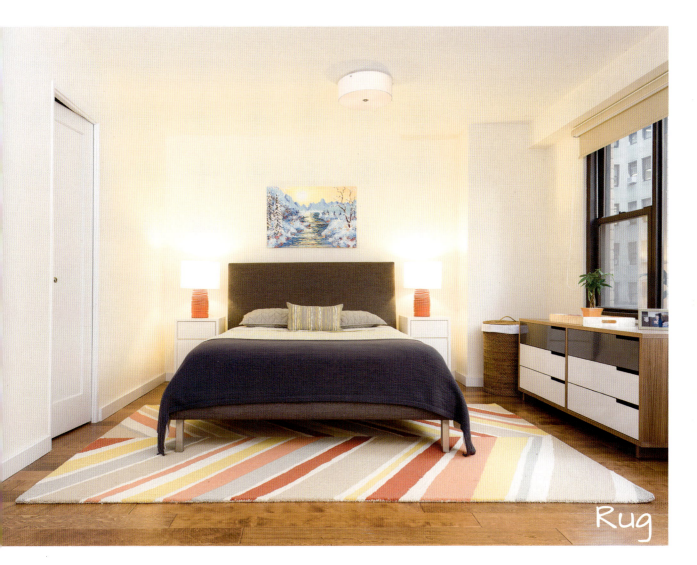

Rug

pete for focus and look like wall-to-wall carpeting that got sliced down the middle. If you don't have enough room to place them at least two feet apart, you don't have enough room for multiple rugs. Stay with the rug in the priority area, typically the seating area, and leave the other area(s) rugless.

- A rug in a bedroom should create a "U" shape at the foot of the bed so that when you walk around the bed, it is plush and warm. In other words, place the rug perpendicular to the bed. It should be roughly 12" in front of the nightstands and centered side to side on the bed. For a queen bed, a 6' x 9' rug is perfect. For a king, 8' x 11' is ideal but rare. So I usually settle for the more common 8' x 10'.

> ## KEEPING IT REAL: WALL-TO-WALL CARPETING
>
> I'm not a huge wall-to-wall carpeting fan. But if you've got it, don't put an area rug on top of it. The plush pile of the wall-to-wall will cause your area rug to shift and bubble up. Not ideal.
>
> The only exception to this rule is if the pile of your wall-to-wall is very low (i.e., commercial-grade carpeting). When placed upon low-pile carpeting, the area rug is less likely to move. When I do layer rugs, I put a slim, rubber mesh rug pad between the two to keep the top one in its proper place.

ENTRY CONSOLES
(Go the Distance)

The Butler of Furniture: This is the piece that greets your guests when they enter your home. It should be stylish, uncluttered, and, most importantly, practical.

Look for:

- **Some flava.** Since this piece is setting your home's first impression, make it a good one. The console should be stylish enough to give a preview of the design to come in the rest of the rooms.
- **A tray to put on top.** Day to day, this tray will be a mail and leash catcher. On special occasions, you can fill the tray with champagne flutes to welcome your guests to your housewarming or with ballots to start the festivities at your Oscar party.
- **Storage.** A tray can't do all your heavy lifting. Mail and a leash? Okay. Umbrellas and spare keys? Too much. Put those items behind your console's doors or in its drawers.

Positioning Pointers:

- Unlike a dining table or desk, an entry console is an ideal dumping ground. We all need a place to drop our day's paraphernalia, so I always try to incorporate one in foyer layouts.
- Nothing should obstruct any door in your home from opening fully, especially not your front one. Ensure your entry console does not stop your door's swing.

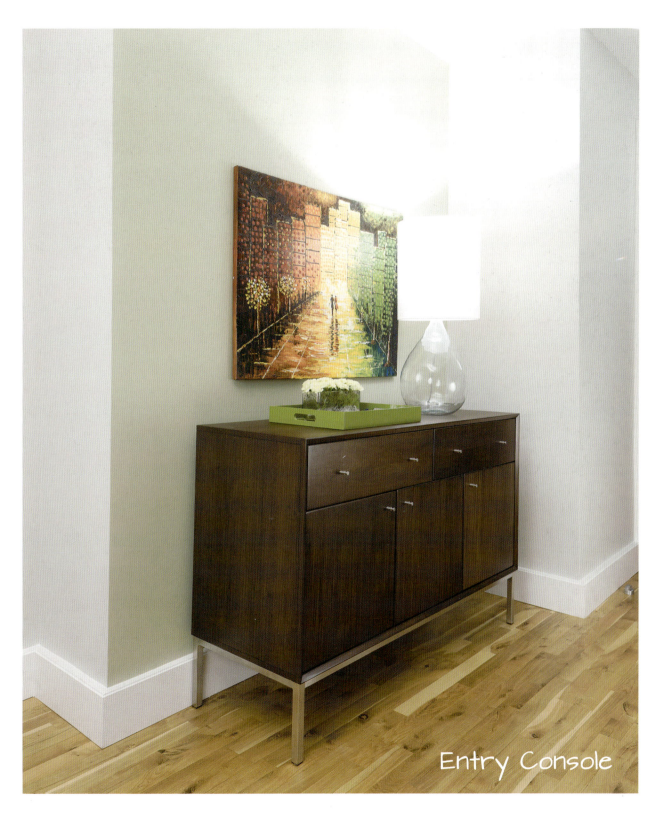

Entry Console

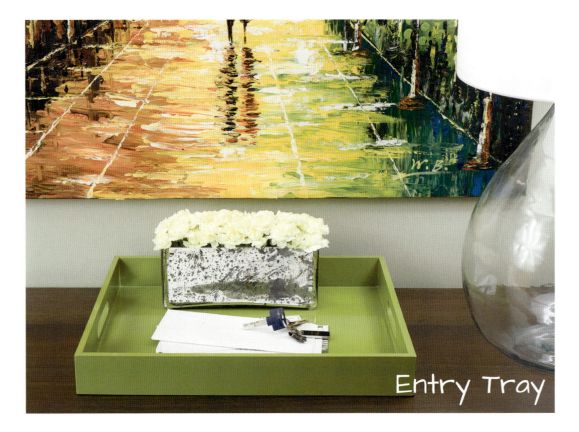

Entry Tray

ENTRY BENCHES (Save)

Let's be under no delusions: With the exception of putting on/taking off their shoes, no one is going to sit here. It is a place for people to put their purse and cast off their coat.

Look for:

- **Durability.** Due to its proximity to the mess of the door, this piece needs to take a licking and be easy to clean. I like leather for its wipeability. A mid-tone color fabric would also work, ideally with a pattern to camouflage stains.
- **Storage.** I like a shelf on bottom for shoes. I like a bench with storage inside for out-door equipment or extra gloves/scarves. You could put a boot tray or baskets under-neath—just be sure they aren't deeper than the bench.

Positioning Pointers:

- The bench should not obstruct the flow into the foyer. No one wants to hit his/her shin, so select one that is slim.

BEDS (Splurge)

This is the piece you will spend the most time on. It is also a piece that doesn't tend to get a lot of rough wear. (I know, there is a joke in here somewhere.) You are probably not going to stain your headboard with spaghetti sauce. Your son probably isn't running his scooter into your bed frame. Make your dreams come true. Spend some cash. Buy a bed you love.

Bed

Look for:

● **Upholstery.** From night-stands to dressers to armoires, bedrooms are generally full of wood. A bed is a perfect opportunity to introduce a new and comfy texture.

● **Its specs.** Most modern beds do not accommodate a box spring. Make sure you check when buying your bed. Because box springs are rarely involved, today's beds are often lower than older models.

● **A queen.** Unless you are living in a dorm or at summer camp, you are not allowed to have a twin or full bed. I don't care how small your bedroom is. I don't care if you are single. Every adult should sleep on a big girl/big boy bed. I lived in a 225 square foot studio for five years and managed to fit a queen bed. You can, too!

- **A king, only if you also have room for significant nightstands.** A king without nightstands is a ship lost at sea. A king bed anchored with appropriately sized nightstands takes a lot of real estate. Make sure your room is large enough to comfortably fit it all. Otherwise, a king makes things too tight.

Positioning Pointers:

- Bed placements share a lot of the same principles as sofa ones. It's usually the biggest furniture piece in the bedroom. Consider placing it on the longest wall first as it will feel most anchored there.
- The bed has more visual impact when placed on the wall kitty-corner from the entry door. With its decadent bedding, accent art, and surrounding lamplight, it is the first thing I want your special someone to see when he/she walks into the room.
- No matter how small your bedroom, a bed with its side pushed up against a wall is never okay. Allow at least a few inches between the wall and the bed for bedding to fall freely.
- Place the bed away from air vents, ac units, and radiators. You don't want to block them nor do you want the air coming from them to make your night's rest uncomfortable.

BOSSY BETSY: BEDROOM CHAIR SMACK DOWN

You may not have a chair in your master unless your bedroom is palatial.

In order for you to actually use it for relaxing, the chair will have to be more comfy than your bed. This means it will need a footstool, a side table for that wine glass, and a task lamp to read by. All of a sudden that small seating nook isn't so little, is it?

If you don't have room for all the aforementioned accoutrements, the bare chair will quickly become nothing more than a dumping ground for clean clothes, dirty clothes, and crap.

NIGHTSTANDS (Go the Distance)

Nightstands are like ears. The face (or bed in this analogy) is the focal point. Guests are checking out the eyes (pillows), makeup (bedding), and hair (headboard). Ears need not stick out as the star. However, they need to be attractive enough to not be offensive, and they sure are fun to bedazzle with interesting earrings (sculptural lamps).

Look for:

- **Storage.** It's always nice to have a drawer or shelf to put things on. However, by now you know that the real reason I want this piece to have storage is to conceal the cords (from bedside lamps, alarm clocks, and phone chargers) that fall behind it.

Nightstand

- **Side tables.** Nightstands are like wedding dresses. Stores mark up nightstand prices. Nightstands are exactly the same as side tables: they both have drawers and/or shelves. They come in the same sizes. Yet, side tables are much cheaper. When shopping for nightstands, I also look at side tables to find a larger selection of price points and styles.

- **The right height.** Measure from the floor to the top of your mattress. Give or take 2″, that is the ideal height of your nightstand.

Positioning Pointers:

- If you are in a couple or single (and looking), two nightstands is best—one on each side of the bed. If you are single (and not looking) or designing a kid's room, one nightstand will do.

- I don't often place a bed on a diagonal for a number of reasons. The main one is what it does to the nightstands. An angular bed placement takes nightstands off the wall, leaving a gap where cords from the lamps and phone chargers become very visible.

DRESSERS/ARMOIRES (Splurge)

Open and shut, open and shut. These pieces get used every day. If the drawers don't glide smoothly or the doors don't close cleanly, you are going to be constantly frustrated. Buy a quality piece that won't drive you crazy.

Look for:

- **Deep drawers.** Shallow drawer dressers are a waste of space. Two pairs of jeans stacked atop each other is a minimum requirement for each drawer (unless we are talking a lingerie chest).
- **Different textures.** Don't be tempted by the simplistic siren song of a dresser set. If you need both a tall and low dresser, get one in a wood tone and the other in another texture, like mirrored or painted wood. (Painted wood doesn't count as a wood tone, remember?)
- **An armoire alternative.** Armoires (free-standing closets) are oppressive beasts that easily overwhelm even large bedrooms. Be sure that you REALLY need the extra hanging storage before you allow one of these monstrosities into your space.

Positioning Pointers:

- In a bedroom, I often use a long-low dresser as a TV stand. Putting or mounting your TV atop is typically the perfect height at which to see it from the bed. Additionally, a place to put a cable box/DVD player/internet TV player is almost always needed. The top of the dresser is a perfect place to put these devices. Some dressers even have slots created for holding these implements.

Dresser

- Tall dressers are the most versatile type of clothing storage. They can move with you almost anywhere. In small bedrooms, I sometimes use one at the side of the bed instead of a nightstand.
- Chunky and clunky, an armoire belongs at the far end of the room so as not to block the open flow into the room.

VANITY TABLES (Save)

It's so lovely and decadent to have a vanity. It's always been a dream of mine to have one, but I have never had a bedroom that is large enough.

Look for:

- **A delicate desk.** There is a very limited selection of vanities. The ones that are out there tend to be expensive. To get a wider breadth of styles and price points, look for a desk instead: more writing desk, less workstation. For the looking glass component, hang a wall mirror above.
- **Good light.** If your vanity is not placed in an area that gets good light, you won't get ready/do your makeup there. Instead, it will serve as a crap collector. Make sure the piece has the right placement for the intended purpose.
- **Storage.** You need to put those brushes, eye shadows, and perfume bottles somewhere. If you clutter them up on top, you won't have a work surface. Look for drawers and/or shelves.
- **A special seat.** You are only sitting here a few minutes at a time. No need for this piece to be super comfy. Whether you choose a tufted stool or a Queen Anne chair, pick an eye-catching cutie whose color/texture contrasts with the vanity table.

Positioning Pointers:

- If you are going to use your vanity table as a place to apply makeup, place it near a window where you can see yourself in natural light.
- Fancy yourself a burgeoning décor expert? It would be adorably asymmetrical to use a dainty vanity table on one side of the bed in lieu of a nightstand.

Now that you are armed with a guide for distributing your budget and creating your layout, it's almost time to hit the stores.

Before you set out on your hunt, we need to get a focused design concept. Thank goodness "Chapter 3: Get Some Style" is only a page turn away!

CHAPTER 3:
GET SOME STYLE

My clients know what they like, and they definitely know what they don't like. However, they have no idea how to focus these ideas into a cohesive vision. That's why they call me. That's probably one of the reasons you are reading this book. If you are nodding your head, this chapter is for you!

Before you can pinpoint your personal style, you have to know how the design industry defines the terms. We want you using the correct lingo, after all.

DESIGN STYLE DEFINITIONS

ASIAN

Elements from Eastern cultures are celebrated in this style. Natural materials like bamboo, rice paper, and silks are mixed, creating a calming and serene space. Wood surfaces are untreated or lacquered. Accents are an assortment of earth tones, metallics, and lucky reds. Detailing often includes Asian symbols or imagery.

Betsy's translation: Day spa chic meets Dojo bold.

BEACH

This coastal style will transport you seaside. It is light, airy, and inspired by all things ocean. Colors closely associated with this style are pale blues, nautical navys, muted corals, sandy browns, and seafoam greens. Whitewashed woods, wicker, and seeded glass are popular furniture finishes.

Betsy's translation: If you don't actually live near a body of water, this can look out of place. Be conservative and tasteful when buying literal ocean imagery and objects to avoid the "theme room" look.

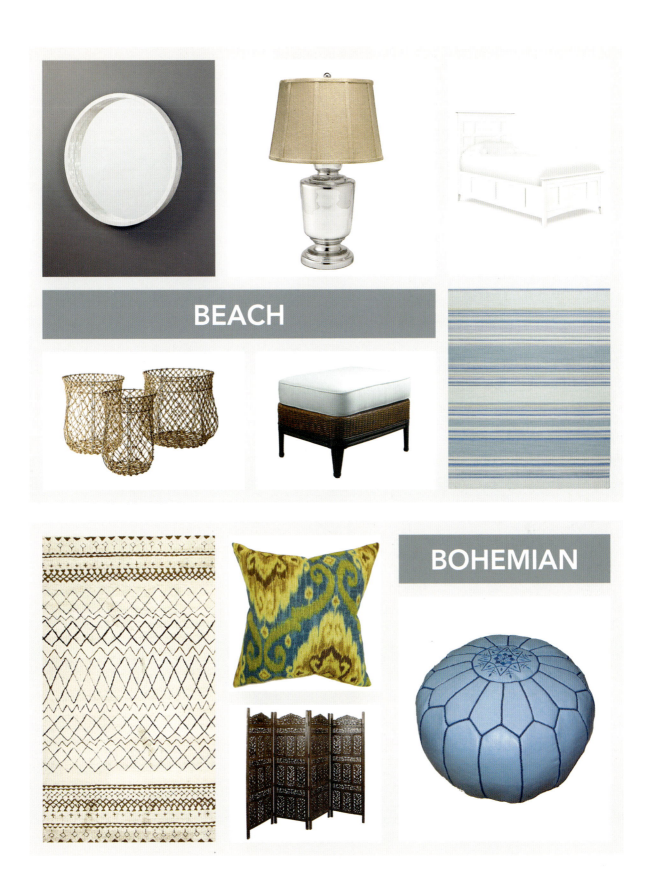

BEACH

BOHEMIAN

BOHEMIAN

Ahh, the life and décor of a wandering vagabond… Spaces in this style are full of accessories, embellished fabrics, and jewel-toned colors.

Betsy's translation: You want a home that embodies your international flair and affinity for the folk arts. Be careful as spaces in this style can start to look like crazy street souks. Find a few inspiration images and edit judiciously to ensure your gypsy mish-mash stays sophisticated.

CONTEMPORARY

By definition, it is whatever is happening "now" in design. Currently, this style is summed up as "less is more," characterized by clean lines, simple shapes, pops of color, and clutter-free surfaces.

Betsy's translation: My clients often make the mistake of using modern and contemporary interchangeably. They are not the same. See below for modern's meaning.

ECLECTIC

ECLECTIC

Whimsical and surprising, eclecticism relies on color, pattern, and texture rather than strict furniture styles to create its cohesive look. These rooms are the epitome of a "mix," blending many styles, patterns, and palettes.

Betsy's translation: You need to be bold to pull this off successfully. Make sure you shop a multitude of stores and feel confident in your vision. Otherwise, you are going to have a hot mess on your hands.

GLAM

A.k.a. Hollywood Regency, this style is all about luxe, shine, and dazzle. From sequined pillows to crystal chandeliers to mirrored furniture, rooms in this style ooze opulence.

Betsy's translation: Make sure you have money to spend. In order to get true glamour, you need to pay. Faux silks and plastic gems will ruin the luxury of this look, and you will wind up looking like a Hollywood wannabe.

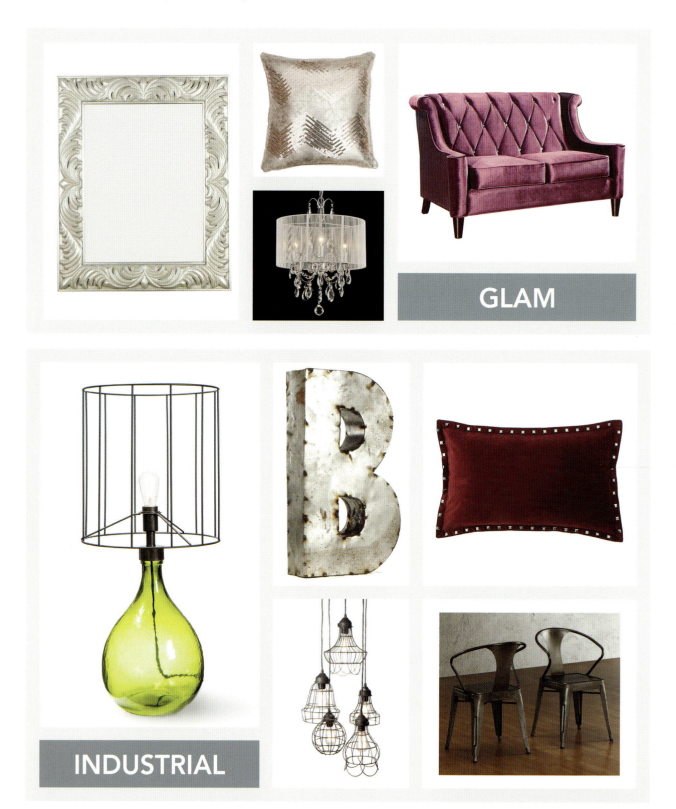

GLAM

INDUSTRIAL

INDUSTRIAL

In New York City, converting old warehouses into lofts is all the rage. The key is to showcase some of the original architectural details: exposed beams, worn brick, uncovered pipes. However, industrial flavor doesn't have to be intrinsic to the architecture. You can introduce this style to any space by selecting pieces fashioned from salvaged materials, incorporating concrete, or mixing aged metals into your décor.

Betsy's translation: This style is dominantly masculine, totally unpretentious, and uncomfortable. Think of ways to soften the look (see the Feeling Words below) so that it feels more like a home and less like a factory.

MEDITERRANEAN

Countries north of the Mediterranean Sea inspire this style. Some refer to it as Tuscan or Spanish Modern. It is characterized by the use of ceramics in pottery and tiles, chunky carved woods, and filigreed metalwork. Stucco and plaster are commonly found textures.

Betsy's translation: This look is big and bold, as is most of the furniture/accents. Make sure you have enough space and gusto to go for these visually heavy and very ornate pieces.

MEDITERRANEAN

MID-CENTURY MODERN

MID-CENTURY MODERN

Inspired by Scandinavian designers and organic shapes, this style originated around the 1950s. Ornamentation is minimal, simple lines are embraced, and jewel-tones like ochre, emerald, and pumpkin are trademarks.

Betsy's translation: If you like the "Mad Men" set, this is the style for you! P.S. It is also the style for me. My clients ask me what my personal style is all the time. I avoid the question; I need to be adaptable and open to every look. But when I shop for myself, Mid-Century with a dash of modern color is where my affinity lies.

MODERN

This style is known for polished and clutter-free surfaces, geometric shapes, and man-made materials (like concrete, chrome, and glass). It takes its name from a 1930s architectural movement.

Betsy's translation: It's easier to admire than live in. Modernism is so sleek and minimal that it can be uncomfortable and hard to find a place for everyday items like mail and toys.

MODERN

ROMANTIC

A very feminine and sensual style characterized by soft textures, low lighting, gauzy fabrics, pastel colors, lace, and curving lines.

Betsy's translation: This style is perfect for the gal in denial: she wants to live in Paris but her boudoir is actually in Boise.

RUSTIC

O Pioneers! Little did you know so long ago that your barn doors and Conestoga wagons would become our farmhouse dining tables and weathered media stands. Spaces in this style feature raw woods, wrought iron, sun-bleached colors, and animal hides.

Betsy's translation: A blacksmith and a lumberjack go into the furniture business and call their store Rustic Style.

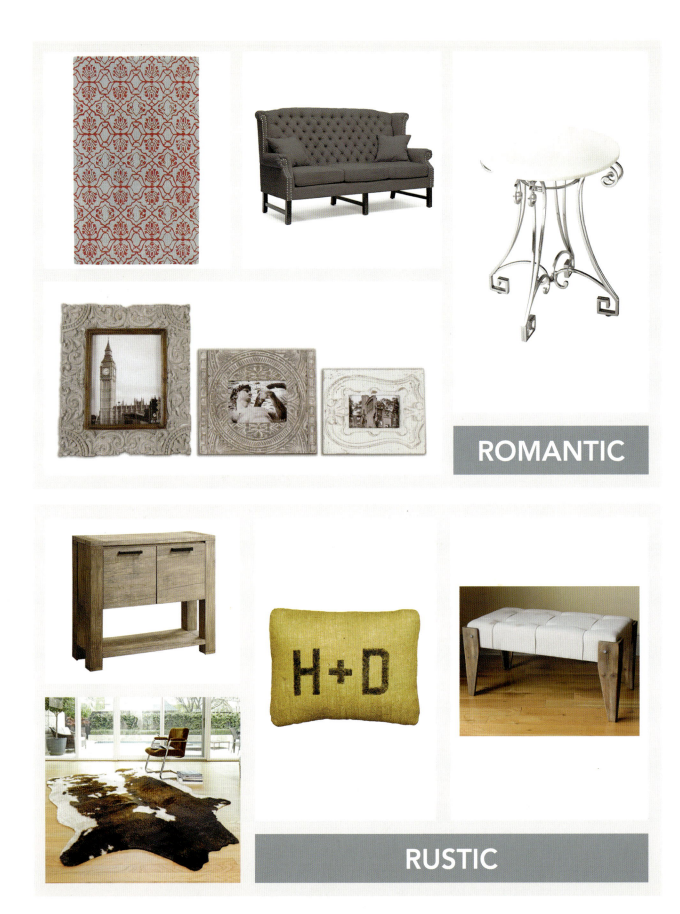

ROMANTIC

RUSTIC

TRADITIONAL

Symmetrical furniture placements, soft textures, and curved lines are cornerstones of this style. This look is timeless, comfortable, and usually neutral or muted in color.

Betsy's translation: Your grandmother would approve of these furniture picks. She may even own similar pieces.

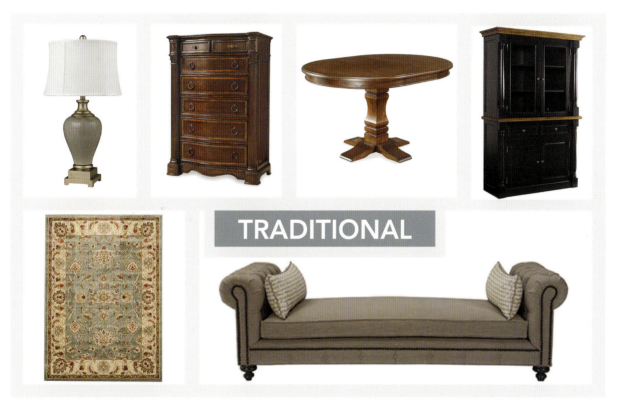

TRADITIONAL

TRANSITIONAL

Think of this as putting a new spin on old classics. It is a blend of contemporary and traditional styles.

Betsy's translation: I call this style "comfy contemporary" or "updated traditional" based on which of the two my client prefers. It's perfect for someone who is tempted by the colors and basic forms of contemporary design but is afraid that sticking with that style will make their place feel too "cold."

TRIBAL

Tribal is a fusion of colors and textures from Africa, Latin America, and Asia. Raw materials and fabrics native to these cultures are mixed to create a globally-inspired, often eclectic space.

Betsy's translation: You have to have an editing eye. Your home shouldn't resemble a souvenir shop in Cancun/Egypt/Tokyo. Overly-international can be unapproachable.

Once you have an idea of the word that resonates with you, you are ready to find your room's specific style. Let's do this!

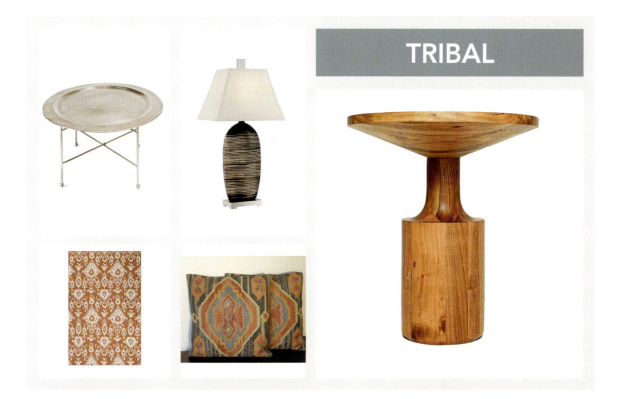

TRIBAL

"BUT, BETSY, WHERE ARE THE OTHER STYLES I LOVE?"

"What about Shaker, Southwestern, or Space Age?" People, my editor is complaining that this book is too long already. I can't cover everything. These are my favorites and the most popular amongst my clients. If you think you might have an obscure style word, do some research online to find one that resonates with you.

YOUR TWO-WORD PHRASE

Now that you know the industry lingo, let's unlock your room's style. All you need are two magical words to get a magazine-ready look. Time to get your chic on with my Two-Word Phrase Method.

For each room in your home, you are going to choose two words. The first is a Feeling Word. The second is a Style Word. The combination of the two is that room's style.

1. **Feeling Word.** The first word should describe how you want you/your guests to feel in the space. Circle the one with the vibe you want your room to exude:
   - Calm
   - Comfortable
   - Happy
   - Formal
   - Energized
   - Cozy
   - Peaceful
   - Playful
   - Edgy
   - Relaxed
   - Sexy
   - Meditative
   - Groovy
   - _____

2. **Style Word.** The second word is the desired style of your space. Circle the style that you gravitate toward:
   - Traditional
   - Contemporary
   - Transitional
   - Modern
   - Mid-Century Modern
   - Asian
   - Romantic
   - Retro
   - Minimalist
   - Glam
   - Bohemian
   - Eclectic
   - Rustic
   - Industrial
   - _____

Now that you have your two words, you are ready to shop. With each piece of furniture or accessory that you consider, ask yourself if it embodies either your Style Word or your Feeling Word. If it fits one of the categories, buy it! If it doesn't fit either word, it's a no-go.

Layer the words throughout the space. When I select a lamp in my client's Style Word, I know I must choose a side table in the Feeling Word. A throw blanket that embodies the Feeling Word should be placed on a sofa that matches the Style Word.

My Edgy Romantic lady (see But Betsy Box) wanted a classic and blingy crystal chandelier hanging above her table (very romantic). Therefore, I knew I wanted the floor rug below it to have an edgy vibe, ergo my zebra choice. Constantly layering your two words through-out the space will give the room a design that is both focused and complex.

LOOK BOOSTERS

OPPOSITES ATTRACT MORE COMPLIMENTS

Kick your design up a notch by choosing a Feeling Word and a Style Word that are nearly opposites of each other. Wouldn't "Cozy Industrial" be great? Cozy is snuggly warm. Industrial is known to be cold and uncomfortable. I love some juxtaposition: a couple of chunky knit pillows tossed into a galvanized metal bucket. Yes, please.

I want to live in a world that gives me a little Energized with my Traditional. I am envision-ing primary-colored paisley curtains hanging behind a trestle dining table. A bright red ottoman would be at the foot of a wingback chair. Now you are thinking like a designer. Contrast is king, my friends.

The more different your two words, the sooner you will be ready for your spread in *House Beautiful.*

IN BED

Want to go beyond *House Beautiful* and shoot for *Architectural Digest*?

When you open a fortune cookie and read the prediction, do you add "in bed" to the end? "You will come into a lot of money—in bed." "Smiling will make you feel younger—in bed." "You will be hungry again in one hour—in bed."

There is a secret word I add to the beginning of all my clients' two-word phases that ensures an amazing look. The third word I add is "sophisticated." Each item I choose needs to be both sophisticated and the feeling or style word.

Sophisticated Cozy Industrial. Sophisticated Energized Traditional. Sophisticated Calm Retro.

Adding that magical word will keep you from getting too kitsch or from being blinded by something that matches one of your two words but isn't a very stylish piece.

You are ready to achieve a professional look—in bed(room)! And in living(room)! Now let's talk color.

Edgy Romantic

"BUT, BETSY, CAN MY ROOM HAVE TWO STYLE WORDS OR TWO FEELING WORDS?"

No. Make your life easy and follow my rules. If you feel there is a word missing or that your room isn't adequately summed up by the two words you have found, you haven't found the right words. For example, I had a client who was adamant that she wanted both a Rock 'n' Roll Style and Romantic Style for her room. She was most excited by the romance idea. That became her style word. For rock 'n' roll, I asked her what that would feel like. She said the room would feel edgy. Aha! Her two words: Edgy (the feeling) and Romantic (the style).

A couple client of mine wanted their living room to have an older feel of bygone eras but also wanted it to feel happy. Old-world was the most important to them and that became the style word. We sprinkled their room with antique-style pieces and distressed woods. Then we kept happy as the feeling word and made sure to use vibrant hues and lively patterns. Their two words: Old-world (the style) and Happy (the feeling).

Old-World Happy

CHAPTER 4:
COLOR DECODED

Don't be afraid, gentle readers. Follow me. Follow me to the bright side of the rainbow. There are magical colors waiting for you. I promise they won't hurt you. I know you are scared. You are not alone. Most of my clients say their biggest design phobia, greater than a fear of blowing their budget or fear of furniture showrooms, is of color.

"BUT, BETSY, I DON'T WANT TO USE COLOR."

"I only want to use neutrals. I saw pics of Keri Russell's house in 'Elle Decor.' She used shades of creams and beige exclusively, and it was so tranquil. I want that."

And I want you to have Keri Russell's budget. But that is not going to happen—and neither is your all-neutral dream. When designing on a budget, you may NOT use only neutrals! Neutrals are defined as colors that you won't find on the basic color wheel: whites, ivories, tans, and grays. They don't catch our attention or create contrast. As such, we look more closely to find visual interest in the small details. When we look more closely at Keri's space, we see textured silks, elegant embroidery, and impeccable stitching.

When we look closely at an affordably designed neutral room, I see stock fabric on sofas, wonky seams on sale pillows, factory-made faux-silk rugs. It doesn't look luxe. It looks boring.

In affordable interior design, we need to draw the eye away from the less-than-impeccable details. We spark interest with contrast and colors—even if they are muted. On board? Great. Let's pick your palette!

USING AN INSPIRATION PIECE

Selecting a color palette with confidence is easy. It's as easy as picking one item that you really like. This beloved piece is called the room's Inspiration Piece. 98% of the time the item is artwork or a textile (i.e., a rug, pillow, curtain, or upholstered piece of furniture). However, it can be anything as long as it meets three requirements.

When evaluating your possible Inspiration Piece, ask yourself these questions to ensure that it qualifies:

1. **Can this piece be placed so that it's seen from almost every angle in the room?** The Inspiration Piece need not be front and center in the space. It doesn't even have to be big. But it does need to be visible from most vantage points in the space so that people visually recognize the cohesiveness of your color palette.

2. **Is this a piece I really like?** Because it is the linchpin of the room's design, everyone who has say over the design of the space should like the Inspiration Piece. If you can see it from almost everywhere, you'd better like looking at it, right?

3. **Does it contain three colors or more?** Three colors is a minimum. By colors, I mean COLORS. Think ROYGBIV (red, orange, yellow, green, blue, indigo, violet) and its derivations. If your Inspiration Piece contains more than three colors, hooray! You have some hues from which to choose.

If you answered "yes" to these three questions, let's make it your Inspiration Piece and use that item to determine the space's color palette. In this case, I used the area rug as the room's inspiration. It is front and center and 8' x 10'. Prominence, check!

My client (and I) really liked its colors and pattern. Beloved, check!

The rug features a bunch of colors, check!

Out of all the Inspiration Piece's colors, select three. Voilà, you have your color palette! In this case, I chose buttercream yellow, sky blue, and chocolate. When I selected an accessory, a fabric, wall paint, or anything colorful for the room, it was one of those three colors: a buttercream side chair, a sky blue throw, a pair of chocolate embroidered pillows.

SPECIFIC SHADES

Buttercream, sky blue, and chocolate. You notice I didn't call the colors yellow, blue, and brown. You need to be specific. You need to repeat the exact same shade of your chosen colors around the space. For instance, I chose sky blue. I can't use navy or royal blue or even a darker shade of sky blue. I need to use the exact same shade of sky blue. The same applies for the buttercream and chocolate.

60/30/10

Remember those three colors we selected earlier—buttercream, sky blue, and chocolate? We aren't going to use those in equal amounts throughout the room. That would be too expected, too formulaic.

We will use one of the colors 60% of the time (buttercream), another 30% (sky blue), and the third 10% of the time (chocolate). In this picture, the buttercream is used significantly more: for the wall paint and side chair. (FYI: Anytime you use a true color like a yellow for wall paint rather than a neutral, that automatically becomes your 60%.) The sky blue is used second most for the throw blanket, the accent pillows, and portions of the diptych painting above the sofa. The chocolate is sprinkled around the room in small doses: the brown and white embroidered throw pillows pillows, the ottoman tray, and certain areas of the painting.

SWITCHEROO

If you have a large room that serves two distinct functions and you want each area to feel a bit different, this is a paragraph you won't want to miss. Say that you live in a studio apartment, and you'd like your living space to have a different vibe than the bedroom area. You will still follow the good ol' 60/30/10 rule. However, in the secondary area, you will switch the colors for the 60% and for 30%. So if you started with teal as your dominate color and purple as an accent, it would be flipped here. The purple would become my 60% and the buttercream my 30% in the secondary zone.

RAINBOW RUNDOWN

Different colors are going to set unique moods and create specific effects. Below are descriptions of each hue to help you when choosing the 60/30/10 palette for your rooms.

CONSIDER THIS: BEND IT LIKE BETSY

Now that you are a color convert, perhaps you are feeling limited by only being able to use three colors? Perhaps you are angling to be designer's pet and want to show me how colorful you are willing to go? (I do have more fun with my colorful clients!) Or perhaps you just have a lot of stuff in a lot of random colors that you don't want to get rid of?

If any of the above apply, you are going to bend the 60/30/10 rule. You are going to stay true to the 60% and the 30%. With the 10%, you are going to sprinkle small doses of any color, as long as it is found within the Inspiration Piece, throughout the room. Yay, color!

RED

RED

Red is an intense hue that arouses a duality of emotions: passion and anger, love and danger. Proceed with caution.

Pros: Use this color to draw attention to something fabulous in your space. Hang red drapes on either side of a window with awesome views. If you have an expensive dining table, show it off by encircling it with red chairs.

Cons: If you have a stressful job (like being an interior designer ☺) or are easily anxious, steer clear of this color as it increases heart rate and can visually overwhelm.

Designer Secret: There is a school of thought in design that believes red is like lipstick on a lady. No room is fully done without one splash of red. No matter their 60/30/10 choices, they always add one red element. I am amused but not in agreement. Rather, I think there is a color further down this list that is necessary for every room. Keep going…

ORANGE

Playful and happy, orange is like a sweet little puppy that needs to be reined in.

Pros: This stimulating color is known to increase productivity. Add touches of this hue to a workspace or home gym to pump up your output.

Cons: More of a fun and youthful color than a sophisticated one, it is ideal for an Internet start-up or for a playroom but not a great choice for a formal living or bedroom area.

Designer Secret: Orange increases appetite. I keep it out of kitchens and dining areas—unless I am working with a super skinny client.

YELLOW

Of the entire rainbow, this color is the most energizing and cheerful.

Pros: Yellow is said to inspire creativity, mental enlightenment, and to encourage sociability. If you are studying for your PhD or want to have friends over for dinner more often, this is a perfect match for you.

Cons: As yellows fade and wear, they tend to look dirty and unpleasant.

Designer Secret: Think of yellow the way you do sunlight: a nice glow warms a room like no other color can (especially rooms that don't get a lot of natural light). Too much yellow or the wrong shade can be irritating and uncomfortable. Sunglasses inside are not okay.

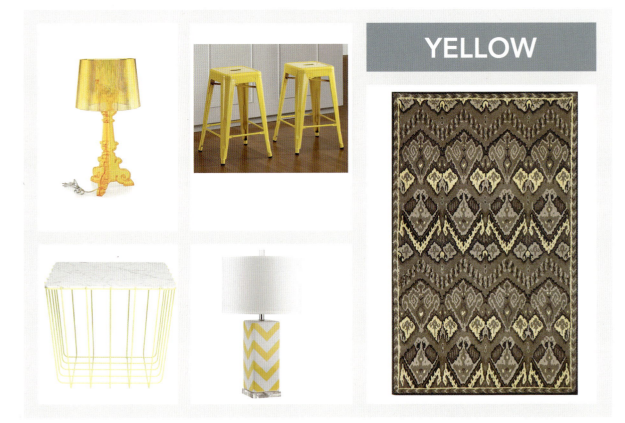

GREEN

From trees to grass to houseplants, green is a color that we associate with security. Day to day we are surrounded by it—we being everyone who doesn't live in NYC where the gray of concrete is the new green.

Pros: Green is at the center of light's spectrum, giving us a feeling of balance when we see it. Use this color in an area where you want to inspire wealth, healing, and serenity. Actors wait in the "green room" before taking the stage as the color is known to calm nerves.

Cons: When choosing a shade, pick one that looks like it could be found in nature. Unnatural shades of green are visually uncomfortable and universally unappealing.

Designer Secret: Green casts an unflattering and sickly glow. I avoid using large amounts of it in rooms where a lot of skin is exposed (i.e., bedrooms and baths).

GREEN

BLUE

Another color that we see regularly when we look up at the sky or down at large bodies of water (with the exception of the Hudson River) is blue.

Pros: Since we are used to seeing large expanses of blue, this color is said to give us a feeling of safety and visually enlarge small spaces.

Cons: Blue can be perceived as cold. Additionally, the color can be so calming that some of its shades often create a tranquilizing effect. This isn't ideal in a home office or hobby room where you need to be productive.

Designer Secret: This color connotes cleanliness. When I come across old bathroom tiling or an outdated kitchen, I use pops of blue in the décor to add a feeling of freshness.

PURPLE

Purple (or violet) is the shortest and last visible wavelength in the color spectrum. As such, it has ties to mysticism, spirituality, and the imagination.

Pros: Purple combines both the serene effects of blue with the passion of red. The color is known to inspire creativity, making it ideal for an art studio or child's room.

Cons: Rarely found in nature, when used in large doses it can feel artificial and uncomfortable.

Designer Secret: Light purple evokes feelings of romance and nostalgia while its darker shades can cause frustration and worsen depression. Because this color is tricky and not universally loved, I use it in small doses.

PURPLE

BECAUSE I'M NICE

Yes, because I am nice and because so many of my clients cling to neutrals like a child with a security blanket, I will let one of your 60/30/10 colors be a neutral. If you selected a neutral for one of your three, it is more important than ever to be specific with that shade. A bunch of browns that are close in color will look like a blah backdrop—not like a design choice.

When working with a shade of brown, caramel and chocolate are strong intentional choices. It is easy to find a variety of objects from many stores in those specific hues.

When working with black, I like a true black, a greige (a mix of beige and gray), or a dark charcoal. And, drum roll, please… You have made it to the color that I think belongs in every room notwithstanding the 60/30/10 picks. I put a splash of true black in each space I design. Black is a mix of all the spectrum's hues. Therefore, it is the deepest color. Having this extreme in one design element (be it as big as a set of dining chairs or as small as a picture frame) puts the room's other colors into context and creates contrast.

According to color theory, white is the absence of color. Unless you are fastidious or have a full-time housekeeper, I don't want you going anywhere near it for your 60% or 30%.

10% pops of white are fine, but I hope for your sanity's sake that they are easily washable. To make white look like a definitive choice, go for stark white or a creamy ivory.

PATTERN PLAY

The palette is set, and we are ready to play. Textiles are the perfect place to have fun and make bold statements with color through pattern. Prints can be found on pillows, rugs, throws, wallpaper, side chairs, ottomans, etc. Combining a variety of them is oh-so designerly. However, they have to play well together. Get your prints to get along with two guidelines:

1. All colors in the pattern must be found in the room's Inspiration Piece. Remember that multicolored item from a few pages back? It sets the parameters for which colors can be featured in your prints. Each print can feature as few as one or as many as all the tones from the Inspiration Piece. However, the pattern may not feature a color that's not in the Inspiration Piece.
2. Each pattern must be of a different scale. Go for an oversized ikat print a large damask, a medium plaid, a small stripe, and a micro-floral. Do as few as two prints or as many as you can find. Just make sure that no two are the same size.

Now that we have picked your 60/30/10 and your fabrics, what color are we going to use on the walls?! Let's turn the page and discuss the most dominant element in any room: paint.

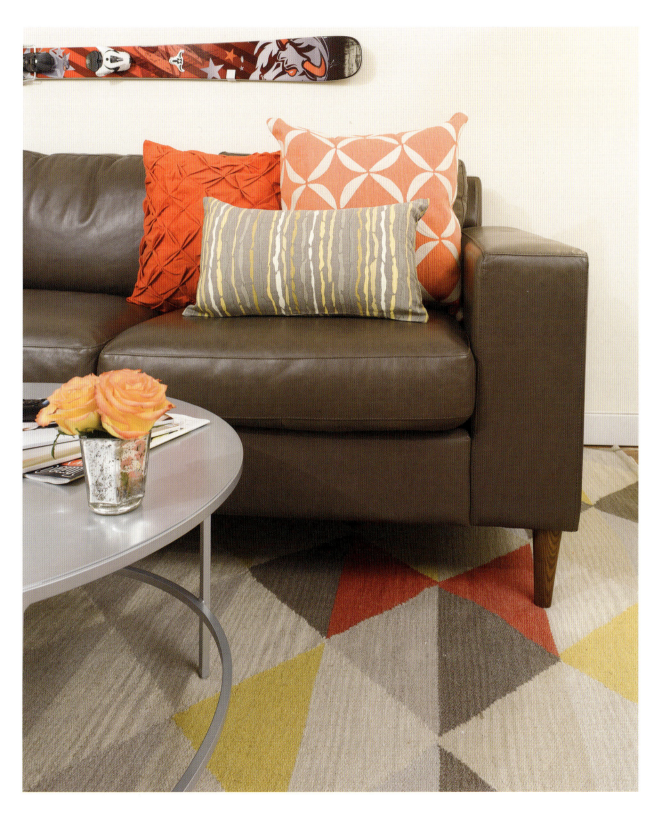

CHAPTER 5:
THE POWER OF PAINT

Choosing a paint color is a big decision. Painting is labor and time intensive. Personally, I would rather be in the dentist's chair than on a ladder with a roller. I pay people to paint, which gets expensive. You don't want to have to do it/ get it done more than every four to eight years. Picking your perfect paint color and finish the first time is imperative. No pressure.

Walking into the paint store and seeing walls covered in colorful chips is daunting. It is even intimidating for me, and I do it several times a month. There are several ways I get in and get out with confidence—and with the perfect color.

SHORTCUTS TO MAKING A SPLASH

MY BUDDY, BEN

First things first, I only buy paint from Benjamin Moore. This company has a great selection of bases. From low-VOC to waterproof to built-in primers to chalkboard paints, they have quality products. I also love them because my clients can easily find a retailer anywhere in the United States. Also, I am a big design magazine and book reader. I love to research and try new colors based on high-end designer

"BUT, BETSY, I AM AFRAID TO ASK: WHAT COLOR SHOULD I PAINT MY WALLS?"

"I am still reeling from your anti-neutral rant in the previous chapter." Readers, this chapter is salve for that wound. I love neutrals—for paint. Love. Neutrals. I don't want you to paint more than every four to eight years. By picking a neutral, you are giving yourself a beautiful canvas on which to splash colorful accessories, fabrics, and art. A subtle wall color allows your accents to sing. I don't want your walls stealing the show.

If you paint with a strong color, you'd better be sure that you are pumped to live with that tone for several years. True confession: I painted my first NYC apartment Pepto-Bismol pink—definitely not a classic color. Not my finest design moment. I had wanted to highlight a bold hue in my Inspiration Piece, a thrift store shower curtain I sewed into drapes. Ahh, youth. Ahh, poverty.

Instead of being wowed, I felt nauseous every time I opened my door. After twelve months in that space, I was desperate to distance myself from pink and I still have a strong reaction to that shade. If I had gone with Pepto throw pillows or a pouf instead, I could have easily swapped the pink out when I was over it. Lesson learned.

recommendations. Most of the colors they promote in those publications are from Benjamin Moore. Lastly, my old boss, Thom, was a huge fan. If it is good enough for J. Lo, it's good enough for my clients!

HC/AC/OC

Not all Benjamin Moore colors are great. 90% of Benjamin Moore's colors are stinkers. They are loud or trendy rather than sophisticated and timeless. When I walk into that paint store, I head straight to a little kiosk in the back. That is where they keep the gold: the Historical, the Affinity, and the Off-White Colors.

The Historical Colors consist of 174 hues that are inspired by 18th- and 19th-century architecture. Rich in pigmentation, these colors are classics.

The Affinity Colors are specifically chosen and endorsed by interior designers and architects. Shopping this section is essentially having a design professional hold your hand at the paint store.

The Off-White Colors are the only place I look when searching for a sophisticated neutral. From baseboards to trim to ceilings to walls, these 140 tones are interesting enough to work in a Connecticut estate, a Hamptons beach house, or a Montana double-wide.

GLOSS-ARY OF FINISHES

At the counter, the paint mixologist is going to ask you which finish you prefer. That refers to the paint's level of glossiness. Here is a guide to getting it right:

FLAT/MATTE

This sheen-less finish (brace yourself for a Charlie joke) is winning on ceilings or on walls. Most of us have walls with patched-over nail holes, textural flaws, or visible sheetrock seams. Flat/matte is ideal for concealing these imperfections. However, it does not hold up well to a lot of wear or repeated washings.

EGGSHELL

This very subtle sheen is barely noticeable, but it will betray the above flaws. If your walls are pretty nearly perfect, use this more durable option all over.

PEARL

Day light or lamplight seems to dance off this more lustrous finish. It can take a licking (or a washing) and keep on ticking. I love it on walls that have no imperfections and see a lot of action (i.e., hallways, family rooms, and playrooms).

I also use this very durable finish in kitchens and bathrooms that are very well ventilated.

SEMI-GLOSS

If your kitchen or bathroom is not well vented, semi-gloss is the finish for you. It resists humidity and stands up to serious scrubbing.

Additionally, I recommend that all trim, moldings, windowsills, and doors be painted in semi-gloss. The contrast between shiny moldings and flat/matte walls is nice. More importantly, sticky fingerprints, boot scuffs, and dust wipe off this finish easily.

HIGH-GLOSS

This super shiny finish creates a lacquered look. In all my years of design, I have used high-gloss less than a handful of times.

I used it when painting a fireplace because the soot scrubs off like a dream. I used it in a Brooklyn brownstone that had hand-carved baseboards and crown that I wanted to show off and make shimmer like freshly fallen snow. Rarely do the spaces I design have something that needs to be hosed down or shamelessly flaunted. I nearly never use this finish and neither should you.

BOSSY BETSY: TEXTURED FINISHES

You know the ones: suede, sand, and crackle to name a few. I didn't discuss them above, and for good reason. Texture is fine if you have walls that are damaged, uneven, or scarred with imperfections. If you have decent walls, don't destroy them with textured paint. It takes a knack (as well as extra time) to apply and is extremely tough to remove. Unless you pay a pro, it usually comes out looking like you should have paid a pro. The same goes for any faux-finish or wallpaper treatment. For the above reasons, I find that these treatments are too labor-intensive and expensive for my clients.

HOME RUN HUES

REDS

Are you sure you want to do this after my Chapter five warnings about anxiety? If you won't be dissuaded, go for:

- Merlot Red, 2006-10—A rich blend of just the right amount of blue and orange, this color looks great in the lightest or darkest of rooms.
- Razzle Dazzle, 1348—You wanted to go there. So we are going there. This hot pink is bold and beautiful.
- Love & Happiness, 1191—A touch of tan grounds this ballet slipper pink.

ORANGES

Deep orange is a tough color to choose and even tougher to live with for years and years. I prefer less vibrant shades like these:

- Jumel Peachtone, HC-54—Peach's perkiness is kept in check with this subdued shade.
- Ansonia Peach, HC-52—This color reminds me of caramelized peaches in a cobbler. (Note to self: Don't write when hungry.)
- Soft Marigold, 160—It casts a bronzed, sunset-like glow on everything it touches. Skip your next spray tan. Just get naked in a room painted in this color.

YELLOWS

Yellow walls wrap around you like a sunny blanket. Here are my picks:

- Powell Buff, HC-35—In daylight, it looks beige. In lamplight, it looks yellow. In any light, it is lovely.
- Straw, 2154-50—Warm up a hallway or living room with this great shade of wheat.
- Mellow Yellow, 2020-50—This practically primary hue is perfect for a lively playroom or home gym.

GREENS

Choosing just the right color is imperative as greens that aren't found in nature can feel uncomfortable and "off." Stick with these shades:

- Hancock Green, HC-117—If you are looking for a real green, this is an unapologetic yet inoffensive choice.
- Aganthus Green, 472—My clients are constantly seeking a sage that isn't too bright or too drab. This is the winner time and time again.
- Gray Cashmere, 2138-60—Subtle like a newly sprouted bud, my favorite greens whisper rather than shout from trees.

BLUES

Let's create your perfect, soothing oasis with one of these cool tones:

- Iceberg, 2122-50—This gray-blue gives walls a silvery shine.
- Beach Glass, 1564—A hint of green softens this inviting blue. It's enchanting and beautifully enveloping, especially in a bedroom.
- Wedgewood Gray, HC-146—Thanks to its deep undertones, this rich baby blue won't read "baby's room."

PURPLES

Sophisticated purple is not an oxymoron if you choose one of these:

- Sanctuary, AF-620—Choose it if you have outgrown a girly princess palace but still want a feminine feel.
- Peace and Happiness, 1380—This lavender is soothing and serene. I love it in a dining room or bedroom.
- Purple Hyacinth, 2073-40—A pretty shade of plum with just enough red to keep things warm and romantic.

BROWNS

Ground your room with the ultimate earth tone. These basic browns are best:

- Papaya, 957—This creamy caramel brown is an ideal neutral in any room.
- Middlebury Brown, HC-68—If a chocolate bar were thrown in a cement mixer, this rich gray brown would be the result. It is classic and a great contrast against stark white moldings.
- Grant Beige, HC-83—Tan, kicked up a notch.

GRAYS

Create a sleek backdrop with just the right splash of gray:

- Horizon, 1478—This pale gray pairs well with any color you choose for room accessories or an accent wall.
- Gray Owl, OC-52—Whoo, whoo doesn't love this greige? It looks lovely anywhere and is one of my favorite neutrals.
- Revere Pewter, HC-172—A rich classic that is great in rooms that get a good amount of natural light.

OFF-WHITES

Instead of blah, a neutral wall paint can create an aha if you pick the right paint:

● Atrium White, PM-13—This warm white is my preferred choice for trim.
● China White, PM-20—A stronger choice for trim is this gray-white—it also happens to be Thom Filicia's molding go-to.
● Ivory White, 925—On walls and trim alike, this buttery white color is always crisp but never cold.

KEEPING IT REAL: ACCENT WALLS

An accent wall is one whose color or design differs from the other walls in the room. Accent walls are non-committal. They reveal that you wanted to use a strong color or design in the room but were too afraid to really go for it. Paint the whole room in that color or don't use it at all—with two exceptions:

1. You may paint an accent wall if you rent. Rentals often require that you bring all the walls in the space back to their original condition when you leave. Paying to have the entire place painted and then repainted is prohibitively expensive. In that case, I am open to painting only one wall. We gotta keep an eye on that bottom line.
2. If you live in a modern space, I will allow an accent wall. Modern architecture often has an open layout, one whose rooms blend into one another without a distinct delineation. I understand not wanting to have a bold living room and hallway and kitchen and foyer.

Additionally, modern homes typically have rectangular and flat walls that are not linked together with ornate moldings like crown. Without continuous decorative trim, distinguishing one wall from another can be a striking look.

When selecting an accent wall, be sure to choose one you want to highlight. By definition, the accent wall is the one people will focus on. I typically pick the longest wall in the space that is not interrupted by too many windows or doors. On that wall, I also put the most aesthetically pleasing piece of furniture (i.e., the sofa or bed).

The Skittles Effect

You have been so inspired by this chapter (remember, I am psychic) that now you want to try a different color in every room. Am I right or am I right!? I'm all for having fun, but let's avoid the dreaded Skittles Effect. Use no more than three paint colors on each floor of your space—one neutral and no more than two ROYGBIV tones. More colors than that and your home becomes a rainbow of fruit flavors.

As an example, let's say you have a neutral living room, purple dining room, and a blue bedroom on your first floor. Fine. But don't paint your hallway green. Too much. If you want something new in the hallway, choose a lighter or darker shade of the neutral, the purple, or the blue used in the surrounding rooms. You can choose multiple colors and still keep it classy.

CHAPTER 6:
WHAT IS ART?

As you know from the Introduction, I started my design career as a painter. It is no wonder that I have a chapter's worth of thoughts and tips on art. Just because you have a low budget does not mean that are you doomed to have bad art. Let me be your docent as we navigate the often gauche and sometimes wonderful world of affordable wall art.

3-D ART

Watercolor

Wood Collage

Painting

3-D VERSUS 2-D ART RULE

There are two types of wall art: 3-D and 2-D.

3-D ART

3-D art has a texture. Paintings are 3-D. When I look at a Monet, I can see brush strokes because the paint comes off the canvas. Watercolors are 3-D. Painted on textured paper, the page curls and undulates as the liquid colors are absorbed. Collages are 3-D as items pasted or adhered to other items create a layered effect.

Never, ever, ever buy reproductions of 3-D artwork. The texture of 3-D art gives these pieces their soul. When you buy a reproduction, the printing press flattens the innate quality of the work. It becomes a bastardization of the original. It looks fake. It is bad art.

With 3-D pieces, the integrity is in the texture. You need to buy an original. Unless you own the original, do not hang a Monet oil painting or a Chagall watercolor. That also means no hanging those museum posters that feature a flat print of a painting on top and text about the exhibit on the bottom. Those are the adult equivalents of dorm art. A definite don't.

I am psychic, remember? I know you are thinking, "Betsy, I can't afford original art. If I could afford a Monet, I wouldn't be checking this book out of the library. I would be calling Thom Filicia."

I hear you, panicked readers. Rest easy. First of all, there are great web resources for buying original 3-D art. I find budget-friendly gems on several art sites. There are people in Wisconsin who are very bored. They are churning out amazing paintings and selling them online for a steal. I modify my search by price point, color, and subject matter. Badabing! Original art collecting is within reach here:

- etsy.com
- saatchiart.com
- ugallery.com
- zatista.com
- lostartsalon.com

2-D ART

Not all of your artwork has to be authentic. You may buy reproductions of 2-D art. 2-D art is a piece that is flat in its original state. When created, it has no texture. Drawings, photo-

graphs, lithographs, and illustrations are a few of my favorite types of 2-D art. I buy reproductions of them all the time.

Andy Warhol's drawings and lithographs aren't limited to soup cans and Marilyns. He has a huge body of lesser-known works that were created to be replicated. Many were commissioned for catalogs or magazines. I love to use his series of shoes near a dressing area, his collection of cats in a family room, his whimsical map of New York City in a bathroom. I love reproduced Warhol!

As long as they don't look over-reproduced (i.e., like they came from a tourist shop), I am a huge fan of photographs. From close-ups of Moroccan mosaics to panoramas of Brooklyn graffiti, go online to an art website and type in a place that is special to you. There are a ton of photos on sale for a pittance from both famous and small-time photographers.

Illustrations are fun and unexpected. I buy a children's book and frame my favorite images from its pages. The *New Yorker* sells its black and white cartoons. There are thousands to choose from so I pick ones whose subject matter corresponds with my clients' jobs/hobbies.

Finding an affordable 2-D art dealer is as easy as opening your laptop. Here are my favorite sites:

- allposters.com
- art.com
- artoftheprint.com
- artstar.com
- society6.com

THINK OUTSIDE THE FRAME

Art schmart. When designing on a budget, let's not limit ourselves to works made by artists. Think outside the frame. If you can hang it on a wall, it is art. Liberating! Let's brainstorm:

MIRRORS

Mirrors are my favorite of all art alternatives. Unlike art pieces that can be costly to frame, mirrors are hard and typically pre-framed. That's a savings right there. Additionally, mirrors aren't

2-D ART

Illustration

Drawing

Poster

Photographs

just pretty, they can also do some heavy lifting in a room. When hung opposite a light source or window, a mirror reflects light to that area of the room. When hung at the end of a hallway or room, a mirror increases perspective, making the space look longer and deeper.

MAPS

A map of a place that you love is immediately personal. I find big maps of small places and little maps of big places most interesting. I am particularly smitten with the vintage pull-down school ones because you can find obscure places, they come in large sizes, and they don't need a frame as they mount from their top mechanism.

SHEET MUSIC

We all have a favorite song. Order its sheet music and frame each page, creating a series over a sofa or down a hall.

FLOATING SHELVES

Perfect for small accents, candles, or special books, floating shelves create a clean surface for display. However, these shelves are not meant to hold a lot of weight so don't overload them with tchotchkes.

MENUS

If you are looking for art in a kitchen or dining room, pick up menus from favorite restaurants or places you've dined while on vacation. Most menus are on neutral-colored paper. Frame them behind colorful mats for a brighter pop.

TEXTILES

You can hang a tapestry or quilt on a rod. You can also buy a bolt of your favorite fabric and put it in a frame or stretch it over a canvas. A word of warning—geometric patterns or stripes show any imperfection in the mounting with a quick glimpse. I prefer an asymmetrical design that gives you a little more room for error.

HOOKS

Do you have an assortment of interesting handbags or hats? Hang hooks in a random formation in a foyer or dressing alcove. You have automatic storage and a showcase for your stylish accessories.

Magazine Pages

Mirror

THINK OUTSIDE THE FRAME

Menus

MAGAZINE COVERS/PAGES

For an Ayn Rand fan, I framed a *Playboy* interview with her in a hallway. For an Internet entrepreneur, I bought old issues of *Byte* magazine and framed the covers that went with the room's color palette.

BASKETS

Coming in all shapes and sizes, baskets work best on a kitchen or dining wall. They are unexpected sculptures that come in cool forms and serve a function, especially during picnics or egg hunts.

CLOCKS

Timepieces make a bold and graphic statement in a home office, are striking above a mantel, and classic in a library. It's a plus that they are also practical!

CONVERSATION PIECES

Putting everyday objects on walls is an unexpected and affordable way to create visual interest. One of my clients needed a place to store his skis so we hung them above his sofa. A film buff wanted to display his old film reels. I mounted a vintage wagon wheel above a buffet. A collection of grandma's kitchen tools became a sculptural installation above a stove. What do you have lying around the house that you could put on display?

HANGING LIKE AN EXPERT

It's not just what you hang, it's also how you hang it. No lopsided artwork on my watch, people. Always use a level with hanging artwork—unless you have significantly sloped floors, like most of my NYC clients. In that case, it is best to measure from the floor to the bottom of both sides of the art to keep it looking straight.

Do your walls and your sanity a favor. Buy a pack of picture-hanging hooks at your local hardware store. These dainty hooks are labeled with how many pounds they can hold. They are super-secure and leave much smaller holes than screws or nails. One hook per piece leads to shifting, uneven artwork. Using two adds security and prevents the piece from moving over time.

Consistently, my clients hang their art too high—even my tiny clients. No matter the height of the ceilings, artwork needs to be hung at eye-level. Humans don't get taller when the walls do, and humans are the ones viewing your art.

Replicate the look of the Louvre, and hang your art at museum height: 59" from the floor to the center of the piece. If I am hanging two pieces one above the other, the center point between them is 59" from the floor.

When hanging artwork above furniture, I put 4-14" between the top of the furniture and the bottom of the piece. Above a sofa, I do 8-12". Above a bed, I prefer 4-8". Above a computer desk, 7-14". When mounting above pretty much anything else (i.e., a piano, buffet, credenza, dresser, entry table, or vanity), I go for 4-7".

Dining tables are a different story. For art behind a table, I put the dining chair against the wall. From the top point of the chair to the bottom of the art, I leave 3-6". This way I guarantee a guest won't ever bump the art when pushing back his or her chair.

When hanging a series of pictures down a hallway or over a sectional, I leave a 2-6" space between them. Less than 2" doesn't visually separate the pieces; more than 6" and they no longer look like they have a relationship.

Speaking of picture relationships, one of the questions I get asked most is how to create a gallery wall. Scroll down, more design gold comin' atcha!

CREATE A GREAT GALLERY WALL

A gallery wall is a grouping of artwork and/or objects. Typically, the formation is organic and asymmetrical. It's not easy to make such an eclectic moment look effortless. Don't worry; I will guide you to success.

1. **Start with a vision.** Consisting of a lot of pieces, gallery walls are visually powerful and attract attention. Therefore, you want to have a reason for creating one. Perhaps you have a lot of art that you have no other place to hang. Perhaps you have a theme you want to repeat, i.e., all family photos, all dogs, all Paris.

2. **Make it odd.** Add up all the pieces you want to incorporate. If there is an even number, ditch one. It will feel most asymmetrical if you use an odd amount of items.

3. **Place the furniture first.** The artwork should integrate and undulate with the furniture it is hung above. Set the sofa, chair, or vanity first. Then build around it.

4. **Jump in.** The more fun you have and visual risks you take creating the wall, the cooler it will look. I cut pieces of giftwrap in the shape of each item I'm hanging. I label the cutouts with a name of each piece so I can keep track of which is which.

5. **Get taping.** I use blue painter's tape to ensure I won't mar the walls. Tape up the cutouts in different configurations. I normally start with biggest piece somewhere toward the middle. Then I work from the center out. Leave no more than 6" between the pieces. The disparate items need a close visual relationship in order to look cohesive.

6. **Picture it.** In between each configuration, I take a photo. With a pic of each one, I feel free to take the groupings down without fear that I will forget my favorite.

7. **Commit!** Pick the pic you like the best. Recreate it. Then hang it or, in my case, pay someone to hang it. Voilà!

You have mastered art in its many affordable forms. Now is the time to reach for your thinking cap. Yes, it is time for window treatments. Cue daunting music…

KEEPING IT REAL: THE CHICKEN TEST

The key to a perfect picture wall is that the pieces stay level in their formation. If even one frame is wonky, the whole vignette looks sad. Only do a gallery wall in an area that won't get bumped. Many of my clients want to hang an arrangement up a staircase or down a hall. I ask that they first take my Chicken Test. Put your thumbs in your armpits and flap your wings while walking on the stairs or in the corridor. If either of your elbows hits a wall, your area is too narrow for picture hanging.

CHAPTER 7:
WINDOW WRAP-UP

Windows. We've all got them. We all need to cover them. Thinking cap on? Let's do this.

BLINDS AND/OR DRAPES

A fully dressed window has both blinds and drapes. It is the chicest and most polished look. With both types of treatments on your windows, you are only meant to close the blinds. The drapes remain open on either side of the window adding texture and color, and visually enlarging the window. The blinds move, the drapes don't.

While it is a very finished look, not all windows need both types of treatments. In modern architecture, like a Tribeca high-rise, having only sleek and minimal blinds fits the style. No need for drapes. If you live in a Connecticut colonial, drapes are a must. The older architecture calls for the more traditional look of a fabric treatment. Blinds are optional.

Of course, the style of the architecture is not the only determinant when choosing treatment(s). There are other factors as well:

- Do you have space above and outside the window molding to hang hardware? Yes, then go for drapes and/or blinds. No, then go for just blinds.

- Do you have a radiator or air conditioner inset in or directly below your window? Just blinds.

- Do you have cats or kids that are curtain-climbing daredevils? Just blinds.

- Does your home feel sterile and in need of color on the walls but you don't want to paint? Drapes are the perfect fix. I add blinds if the room is also in need of texture.

- Do you have a lack of art but want to add visual interest to your walls affordably? Drapes to the rescue! Blinds in addition are a bonus.

- Do your windows swing open toward the inside of the space? Drapes.

- Do they swing open outside? Blinds and/or drapes.

- Do they slide side-to-side or up-and-down? Choose either.

BOSSY BETSY: NO WHITE WINDOW TREATMENTS

Drapes are tough to clean. Some can be dry-cleaned. Some can't. Some blinds can be dusted and wiped. Some can't. Most of the windows I dress are in NYC where our sills are covered in black smog particles. White or cream window treatments show every speck of that soot. They are not an option in an urban environment. Even in rural Vermont, windows are a barrier between our home and the wild 'n' dirty outside. Gray, beige, or anything darker will look cleaner longer.

BLINDS:

Best: Roller

Best: Wood Slat

Best: Fabric Roman

Best: Bamboo

Rest: Metal Slatted

Rest: Vertical

BLINDS: THE BEST AND THE REST

You already know I don't use the "C" word. No custom blinds for my clients—too expensive, too long a wait to get them installed. Below I outline some of the most common retail options for blinds and their pros/cons. I define them by "Best"; these are my top picks that I rely on like trusty friends when treating windows. And the "Rest"; sure, lots of stores sell 'em. But I refuse to use 'em, except in extenuating circumstances.

WOOD SLAT BLINDS (Best)

Pros:

- They are easy to dust.
- Perfect for controlling light and privacy, you can angle the slats to adjust to the time of day/your activity.
- They come in lots of wood tones and some colors. If going for a wood, I choose ones that most closely match the hardwood flooring. If the floors are carpeted, I match the tone I am using for the wood furniture in the space. When going with a color, I coordinate with the room's trim color.

Cons:

- They are a basic, more traditional/transitional look. No wow factor and not the most modern choice.

ROLLER BLINDS (Best)

Pros:

- From blackout to translucent, these blinds come in lots of different opacities, making them versatile for a variety of rooms.
- Most of the textures available are easy to wipe down.
- Slim and minimal, these are ideal in a modern-style space.

Cons:

- Cheap versions of these often look very cheap. Spend a little more for a sophisticated material.
- They are too sleek looking for an older-style home.

FABRIC ROMAN BLINDS (Best)

Pros:
- The perfect hybrid of colorful drapes and clean blinds.
- Choose from a variety of colors and patterns, many with the option for a blackout liner.
- The thicker, lined options keep out drafts and keep in heat/cooling.

Cons:
- Retail sizes are limited.
- Very few provide partial translucency. It's either open or closed/full light or full dark with these beauties.

BAMBOO ROMAN BLINDS (Best)

Pros:
- These are the most affordable of all retail blind options.
- They come in a variety of opacities from translucent to blackout.
- They come in a variety of wood tones from light tortoise to espresso.
- They are a duster's dream.

Cons:
- What's not to love!?
- Okay, one little thing: They don't keep out drafts as well as their fabric cousins.

METAL SLAT BLINDS (Rest)

Pros:
- If you love the sound of screeching aluminum and the sight of blinds covered in cat hair (static cling issues), these are for you!

Cons:
- They are ugly and annoying. Don't. Just don't.

VERTICAL BLINDS (Rest)

Pros:
- If you need to cover a patio door or backyard door, these are a functional and affordable option.

Cons:

- If you don't need to cover a door, there is no reason to choose these.
- The flapping, gangly slats fall out over time.
- Their look is dated.
- Ack!

PLEATED HONEYCOMB (Rest)

Pros:

- They allow light to pass through while still providing privacy.
- These energy-savers help cold to stay out or in, depending on the season.

Cons:

- The honeycomb/cellular construction makes them very tricky to clean. They look dirty and dingy quickly.

TOP-DOWN BLINDS (Rest)

Pros:

- They are the ideal solution if you live in a garden-level apartment or on a street that gets a lot of traffic. You need privacy while still wanting natural light.

Cons:

- They obstruct almost all of your view of the outside while obstructing an outsider's view of you.

INSIDE VERSUS OUTSIDE

After you select your style, you need to decide if you want inside or outside mount blinds. If you have space inside your window box between the panes and the outermost edge of the box, then I'd suggest an inside mount. It is a cleaner look and, when closed, the blind falls neatly in the window encasement. I hang the inside mount blind about 1-2" in front of the window inside the box.

Outside mounts are affixed to the outside of the window. Unbound by the window box, they protrude in a bulky and unflattering way. I only use outside mounts if there is absolutely no room inside the window encasement.

Measuring for blinds can be tricky. For inside mounts, you usually measure inside the window box width-wise and length-wise. If your window is very wide and comprised of multiple panes, get one blind per pane, measuring each pane's width.

For outside mounts, I measure outside the window's moldings for the width and length of the blind. When closed, the blind fully covers the window and its framing. Never drill into the window's moldings. Unlike walls, which can be easily patched, drilling into moldings ruins their integrity, and it looks amateurish.

The above is a general guide. Each retailer's system can be a little different. Look in their info for a measuring guide to see if their process deviates from the norm.

DRAPES: THE BEST AND THE REST

I've got a crush on curtains. I just love 'em! I use colorful and texturally interesting drapes whenever possible. In addition to their visual appeal, when drawn, they are energy-efficient and help keep out unwanted light and sound. There are a lot of styles available (see below). No matter which drapes you choose, thaere are general guidelines to keep in mind.

Firstly, drapery should be hung outside and above the window molding. I hang drapes 2-6" above the window's frame and 4-10" outside. By hanging them higher, they lead your eye up, adding height to your space. Hanging them outside ensures that the drapery won't encroach on the window's light. Additionally, it makes your window look wider. However, don't hang your hardware so far out that the panel doesn't cover the window's

"BUT, BETSY, WHY DO I NEED SO MUCH FABRIC?"

"If I use them with blinds, my drapes aren't really going to close. You said so yourself."
Good question, skeptical reader. You don't want a huge window to be flanked by skinny strips of fabric. They will look disproportionately anemic and definitely not luxe. However, rather than double-width, I am also open to 1.5 times the width of the window in drapery. You'll still get the proportionally thick look without such a hefty price tag. See, I'm open to compromise.

Best: Grommet

Best: Pinch Pleat

DRAPES:

Rest: Tab Top

Rest: Rod Pocket

framing. You want it to cover the window box by about 1" and gently undulate out toward the end of the rod.

The drape needs to brush the floor or extend 1" past. Drapes that extend more than 1" on the floor are said to "puddle." Having yards of fabric on the floor befits a chateau in France or a plantation home in the South but is not ideal for anything less opulent. Additionally, all that extra fabric is a trap for dust bunnies.

On the other side of the coin, drapery that doesn't reach the floor looks like ill-fitting capri pants for your window. It completely negates the dramatic effect of making your space look higher. If there's a reason your drapery can't extend to the floor, blinds are your best bet.

If you were to pull your drapes, you don't want them to be tight and taut. You want them to undulate gracefully. Therefore, you need to double the width of your window in drapery. If you have a 40" wide window, you need 80" of drapery width. That's two 40" wide panels. If you have a very wide window like 100", you need 200" of drapery. There is a very limited selection of drapes that are that wide. They are called doublewide drapes and will cost you an arm and a leg. Instead, I buy four standard-width panels and have my local drycleaner sew each set of two together, creating the same size as a doublewide for a much better price.

PINCH PLEAT (Best)

Pros:

- The most elegant of the retail drapery options.
- They move back and forth easily with rings or on a track.

Cons:

- They can't be used alone. You have to purchase rings or a track to use them.

GROMMET (Best)

Pros:

- Remember my drapery crush? This type of panel is my George Clooney. My Brad Pitt. My Daniel Day-Lewis. I rarely cheat on this handsome panel type with any other model. It is the best.
- Buy it, and put it up on a rod. No other hardware needed.
- It moves back and forth on the rod with ease (yes, I am aware and in support of this double-entendre).
- When drawing closed or pulling open, the panel stays where you put it. No bulky bunching. No push back—just like a good man.

Cons:

- Grommets are an informal choice. They are fine for a normal dining room or living area, but any room that has the word "formal" before it should opt for pinch pleat.

ROD POCKET (Rest)

Pros:

- You will find the most affordable and widest range of styles of these drapes.

Cons:

- They are a nightmare, and I very rarely use them. They fit onto the rod too tightly, making them nearly impossible to draw and close with ease.

TAB TOP (Rest)

Pros:

- The sewn top tabs make the panel easy to push back and forth.

Cons:

- The tabs bunch up together creating a bulky and unsophisticated look when open.
- The tabs are a very casual look that is too informal for many spaces.

HARDWARE:

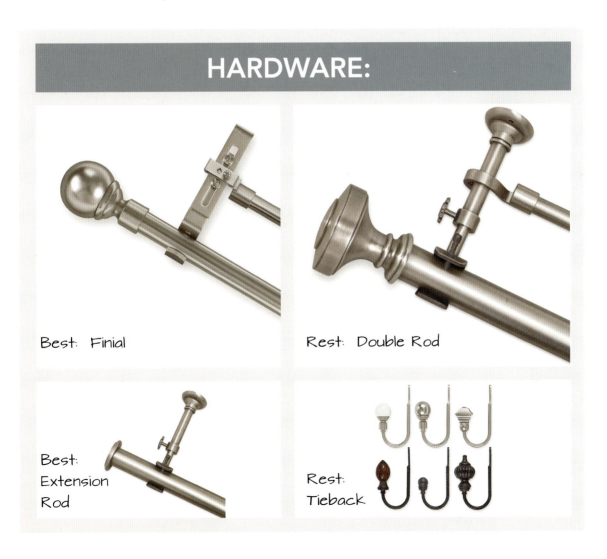

Best: Finial

Rest: Double Rod

Best: Extension Rod

Rest: Tieback

HARDWARE: THE BEST AND THE REST

I like to think of hardware as the male partner in pairs figure skating. (Hardware is only an interesting topic if you use a fun analogy.) It should be there to support the elegant and eye-catching female (a.k.a. the drapes) but not steal her show. I like a strong, unadorned hardware set that makes a clean statement.

EXTENSION RODS (Best)

Pros:

- There is a range of price points, sizes, and finishes available. Select a finish that coordinates with the metals of the home's architecture (i.e., the doorknobs, hinges, and light fixtures).

Cons:

- Skinny rods look cheap and flimsy. All rods should be at least 1" in diameter.

FINIALS (Best)

Pros:

- They are a must as they screw into the side of the rod, preventing it from slipping out of its bracket.

Cons:

- Stick with plain cylindrical finials or, if you must get fancy, round balls. Decorative end caps, like the ones with swirls, twirls, pinecones, or crystal orbs, are too much.

DOUBLE RODS (Rest)

Pros:

- You can hang both a drape and a sheer while mounting only one rod rather than two.

Cons:

- I rarely use a double rod because I rarely use a sheer. When looking for the translucency or partial privacy of a sheer, I opt for a blind instead.

TIEBACKS (Rest)

Pros:

- Remember those unwieldy rod pocket drapes? Swagging these panels behind a tieback is the best way to wrangle them.

Cons:

- When you swag a panel behind a tieback, the drape blocks part of the window, reducing the amount of light the room receives.

Now that our windows are fully dressed, we can take these pesky thinking caps off. Let's stop measuring and resume having fun. It's time to add some bling!

"BUT, BETSY, DID YOU MISS SOMETHING?"

"Did you miss something? Where is the paragraph about valances? About sheers? About tension rods?" No worries, dear readers, I didn't omit them. Turn to pages 152 and 153 to get the scoop.

CHAPTER 8:
THE WOW FACTOR

The right furniture in the right places helps your home look put together. That's nice and all, but we can do better than put together. Let's go for The Wow Factor. I want your guests to gasp, "Where did you get that?" "This room is so inviting!" "Who did you hire?"

ROOM JEWELRY

Get the gasp by adding accents or, as I fondly refer to them, room jewelry. These items are the finishing touches that enrich a room's style, add personality, and create visual interest. Let's start with three general accessorizing tips:

1. Better to be odd. Objects are more interesting when grouped in odd numbers. You'll recall from the art chapter that picture walls look most organic with an odd number of pictures. Groupings that are odd are unexpected, asymmetrical, and more visually interesting. I stack five books on a coffee table—not four. I place three vases on a bookcase—not two. I fill a centerpiece bowl with 13 pieces of fruit—not 12 or 14.

2. Make it a mix of personal and generic. When styling the top of a side table or shelves on a bookcase, I use a mixture of personal and generic accents. If every item on your bookcase has personal significance (i.e., your grandmother's candy dish, clay pots made by your kids, or a trophy from your office trivia night), your room will look like a curiosity shop or a diary come-to-life rather than an inviting, approachable space. On the other hand, avoid buying all your accents retail. Resembling a home staged for sale or a hotel, these items have no backstory or personal connection, leaving your space devoid of soul.

With every surface I accessorize, I actively think about mixing pieces that are personal next to pieces that are generic. On a side chair, I place a client's special teddy in front of a silk pillow I got online. Metal vases flank either side of an oyster shell photo frame featuring a pic of a beach picnic.

3. Think design on vacation. Many of my clients complain they don't have any personal accessories. Never fear. Hop in your car or jump on a plane, and pick something up on a trip. It can be as pedestrian as a vintage coffee tin from Indiana or something more eclectic like a wooden mask from Mozambique. When you find an accent on a trip, there is instantly a memory attached to it.

4. Size matters. As your friendly designer, of course I have a criterion for the piece you find. In order to qualify as an accessory, the item you find must be between 6-20" high. Anything smaller than 6" is not an accent. It is a dust collector, a tchotchke, a piece of crap. It doesn't have visual impact. From a few feet away, your guest can barely deduce that it is there at all. Anything larger than 20" is too big to be a mere accent. It starts to dominate rather than enhance a room. That is fine if you want the piece to be your room's Inspiration Piece. However, it doesn't work if you merely want to integrate the item into an existing scheme. Rule of thumb: if it doesn't fit in your carry-on, it is too big to be an accessory.

LIGHT IT UP

What good is an accessorized room if you can't see when you're in it? Lighting is key to creating a dramatic and livable space.

LOOK UP

Overhead fixtures are practical as they illuminate a room without taking up floor/surface space, but their light is harsh and unrelenting. To soften the unflattering glare, I put all overheads on dimmers. A 15-minute trip to the hardware store to buy a dimmer pack and 15-minute visit from a handyperson can make any overhead light in your home an adjustable one.

When choosing your fixtures, coordinate with the style of the other architectural features in the home like the hardware in the kitchen and bath. If you own, be sure to splurge, as your fixture selection will affect your resale value. If you rent, don't spend a lot as they will most likely not move with you.

Tempted by the dramatic look of a pendant or chandelier in an entryway or above a bed? Be sure your ceilings are 9' or higher. Anything lower than that will be an annoying head-bumper rather than a beauty. If you are hanging a light over a dining table, you don't

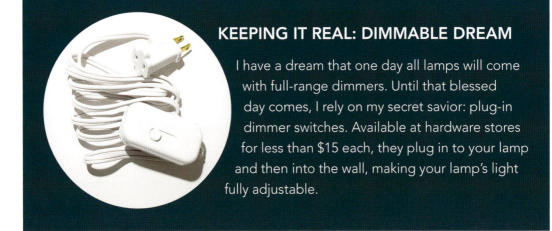

KEEPING IT REAL: DIMMABLE DREAM

I have a dream that one day all lamps will come with full-range dimmers. Until that blessed day comes, I rely on my secret savior: plug-in dimmer switches. Available at hardware stores for less than $15 each, they plug in to your lamp and then into the wall, making your lamp's light fully adjustable.

need to have 9' ceilings. However, you do need to leave 29-32" between the bottom of the fixture and the top of the table.

If you want the effect of an overhead but don't have electric in your ceilings, opt for an arc lamp. Above a dining area, I swoop it from the corner up and over so the shade is centered on the table. In a living room, the lamp's shade floats above the coffee table.

LOOK AROUND

I never rely on overhead lights to illuminate a room. Floor and table lamps create warm pools of light that illuminate the different zones in a room. Every room (with the exception of the kitchen and bath) needs a minimum of three lamps dispersed around the space to create an inviting and well-lit environment. Lamps not only light a room; for those of us who have a limited fine art collection, they are also our sculptures. They add lovely lines, textures, and height.

When shopping for lamps, I keep a couple of things in mind. Firstly, I always look for 100 watt or 150 watt capacity. Anything less is not a lamp, it is a candle. I will sometimes use one that is below 100 watts in a room, but I don't count it toward one of the required three.

Secondly, you have to pay attention to height. Your table lamp's height should be within 2" of the height of the surface it is on. The bedside lamp should be roughly the height of the nightstand; the buffet lamp should be about the same height as the buffet; the side table lamp should be very close to that of the side table. You get the picture.

Floor lamp heights are fairly standard. I add a floor lamp whenever I want to illuminate a larger area or whenever a room could use a boost in visual height.

STILL LIFE

Lamps are not the only affordable sculptures in a room. Plants, our oxygenating friends, are Mother Nature's statues. However, these leafy lovelies can get costly if you can't keep them alive. I only buy ones that are tough to kill. These hearty picks are my seven favorite flora:

DIEFFENBACHIA

This lush beauty features leaves in both green and white. Needing little light and water only once a week, get a tropical look without a big time-commitment.

DRACAENA

I prefer the "Janet Craig" varietal of this plant which actually thrives with mild neglect. Put this tall beauty in indirect sunlight and only water it when it feels dry. Now that's a maintenance plan I can get behind.

JADE PLANT

All this plant needs is bright light. Keep it small or pot it to grow nearly 6' tall. Similar to a cactus, it needs very little water. Additionally, in Chinese culture, this plant is the ultimate symbol of prosperity.

LUCKY BAMBOO

Not bamboo at all, this plant is actually a lily. When kept in water (no soil needed) and low light, it can grow to nearly 8' in height. Fun fact: the number of stalks you display has meaning: three stalks for happiness, five stalks for wealth, six stalks for health.

Lucky Bamboo

Dracaena

PLANTS

Money
Tree Plant

MONEY TREE PLANT

These trees come in heights of small to tall and are said to bring good fortune. They need moderate light and should only be watered every two weeks. I forgot all about my money plant while preparing for my wedding and on my honeymoon. Three weeks later, I returned home to find it thriving.

PHILODENDRON

Don't get a lot of natural light? This plant is for you. Only water it after it completely dries out. In other words, set it and forget it! Put it on a bookcase or drape it over a dresser, and its stems will cascade down.

ZZ PLANT

Water this low-maintenance lovely once a month. Gotta love that. And keep it out of direct light. Another perk is that the ZZ plant is flowering. The blooms are shades of yellow or gold and usually appear in the mid-to-late summer or fall.

SUPER-SECRET SEVEN

Now that you have nearly finished this revolutionary book and your space is almost fully designed, you are ready for my Super-Secret Seven.

I am about to share with you something I have never revealed to anyone. Really. Secretly, before I complete a space, I ask myself seven questions. If the answers are all "yes," I know the design meets pro-standards. If even one of the answers is "no," I know I have more work to do.

Refill your adult beverage, find that pen from Chapter 1, and get ready to check some boxes. This is your home's final exam.

Does each room feature:*

I. Colors (three or more)?
    - No. Take a sip of chardonnay (you didn't know this was also a drinking game), and go back to Chapter 4.
    - Yes. Continue with the list.

---

*The first four were inspired by TLC's *What Not to Wear*. Years back, I was watching the show, and Stacy and Clinton's "Color, Texture, Pattern, Shine" mantra resonated with me. It's a great formula for fashion and (with a few added elements) works for interior design, too.

2. **Pattern (two or more)?**
   - No. Another sip and a slap on the wrist. Didn't you just review Chapter 4?
   - Yes. Continue with the list.

3. **Texture?**
   - No. Go out and get a velvet pillow, a cashmere throw blanket, or some linen drapes. You need one or two things that are fun to touch.
   - Yes. The force is with you. Continue on, Jedi.

4. **Shine?**
   - No. Really? Are you sure you don't have something metallic or iridescent? No mirror, no lacquer? Then no dice.
   - Yes. The bling has been brung.

5. Life?

- No. Every room needs one living element. It can be a plant in a window box, a vase of fresh flowers, a centerpiece bowl with oranges, a cat curled on an ottoman. Pot something, fill something, adopt something, and come back to the list.
- Yes. Water something, eat something, feed something, and continue down the list.

6. Chi?

- What the heck is chi? Every room needs a few areas that are left unadorned. Empty spaces allow good energy (chi) to circulate, the eye to rest, and accessorized areas look more interesting by comparison. Does your room have at least two blank walls or open surfaces? No. Throw a couple of things out.
- Yes. Continue.

7. Something Black?

- No. You knew this was coming. I told you on page 83. Bad designer. Bad.
- Yes. You have aced this. Your space is awesome, Affordable Interior Design-worthy, and magazine-ready. How does it feel? Congrats!

I am puffed up like a proud mama. Eight chapters of tips and tricks and you have mastered them all. I hope you will send me stories of your retail triumphs, regale me with emails of your color adventures, and astound me with your "after" pics. I can't wait!

But… before you go, I have a few last tidbits. Turn to Chapter 9 so I can tell you some final things before you head into the wild world of home décor.

CHAPTER 9:
BEFORE YOU GO

KIT MUST-HAVES

You need the right tools to get your job done. Here are the things I keep in my install* kit:

1. BAND-AIDS

Accidents happen: a baggie of these along with a small tube of Neosporin gel is a must.

2. BRAWNY HANDYMAN (OR TWO)

I fancy myself handy; I was a Campfire girl after all. But I know my limitations. Getting affordable furniture built properly is the key to its stability. Getting art hung by a pro is the key to its visual impact. Plus, I need assistance with the heavy lifting. I throw some money and a few good men at these problems. While they don't technically fit in my kit, they usually carry it for me.

3. CANDLES

What place doesn't look better by candlelight? I love to sprinkle a few votives around each room before my design reveals.

4. CLEAR PACKING TAPE

From binding broken down boxes to packing returns, this tape is invaluable on my installs.

5. DESIGN MAGAZINES

Even I get stuck. When styling a built-in bookcase or arranging vases on a credenza, sometimes I need a little inspiration. I open up the latest issue of *House Beautiful*. While taking a little breather, I also scour its pages for an arrangement I can imitate.

6. FROG TAPE

Forget the blue stuff. This green tape is the only kind to use to get a perfectly clean and straight line when painting stripes or around moldings.

7. GOO GONE

Why do retailers put those super sticky labels on the glass of the picture frame or on the bottom of every tumbler in a set? I have lost years of my life scratching those things off with my fingernail. Goo Gone takes the pesky tags away with a few wipes.

---

*Install is designer speak for the big makeover. It is the on-site process of transforming my clients' spaces. My handymen and I "install" the new items, assemble the furniture pieces, hang the art and window treatments, and make the magic!

8. HAMMER

I leave the complicated stuff to my handymen. But that doesn't mean I don't need a hammer. Every now and again a nail needs my attention to put in or take out. I'm always at the ready.

9. LEVEL

Levels don't ensure that your pictures will look straight when hung above furniture (see page 110). However, when hanging a piece on a wall above nothing, I use both my eyeball and my level to get it right.

10. LIGHTER

I need to light the votive candles with something.

11. LINT ROLLER

The fastest way to remove sock lint, pet hairs, and tiny Styrofoam packing pieces from furniture and rugs is with this trusty tool.

12. MEASURING TAPE

All you really need to be a designer is a 12' measuring tape—and this book, of course. A thin-ish one is better than a heavy-duty version as it has a gentler touch and isn't as likely to snag upholstery or scratch hardwood floors.

13. MINI-SPEAKERS

When my team starts to drag, Michael Jackson, Jason Mraz, and Lady Gaga are our go-to motivators. A charged phone paired with my mini-speakers keeps us upbeat and on track.

14. MR. CLEAN'S MAGIC ERASER

What can't this miracle sponge do? I use it most to take scuffs off wall paint and moldings. It also helps remove sticky price tags, fingerprints around doorknobs, and surface scratches from floors.

15. PURDY PAINT BRUSH

I always ask my client to set out a small can of touch-up paint on install day. A 1.5" brush hits places I've spackled or fixes questionable paint jobs. I love Purdy's multipurpose brushes as the bristles don't shed, and they wash up like a dream.

16. PAINTER'S TAPE

The name of this tape is deceiving because I never use it when painting (see Frog Tape above). Instead, it marks places on walls and floors where my handymen should hang/place things. As you'll recall, I also employ it when creating gallery walls.

17. POCKET DECORATOR BY PAMELA BANKER

When I need a refresher on technical design lingo, this mini-encyclopedia is my personal professor.

18. PROFESSIONAL PICTURE HANGERS

I prefer not to use nails or screws. I go pro when picture hanging and spend more on those awesome hooks.

19. READY PATCH SPACKLE

Spackle is a putty used to repair wall imperfections. Every project presents a few holes to patch. Of all the brands of spackle, this is the kind to have. It dries the fastest, sands the easiest, and won't shrink on you.

20. SANDING BLOCK

For a seamless finish after you spackle, give the dry surface a light sand before painting. A block is easier to hold, control, and pack in my kit than flimsy sandpaper.

21. SCISSORS

I have a utility knife phobia. I use scissors for everything from popping open boxes to cutting flower stems to taking off tags.

22. SCREWDRIVERS (FLAT AND PHILLIPS)

Fancy electric options are nice. But I can't get through even one install without reaching for my old-school screwdrivers. Sometimes the manual way is the best way.

23. SCREWS AND ANCHORS

I keep extras of these in several different sizes to hand to my handymen when they run out. These are for the harder-to-hang items like drapery rods and for affixing tall furniture to walls.

24. SEWING KIT

Whether it's loose buttons on duvet covers or over-stretched pillow seams, I'm always glad I have a needle and thread.

25. SHOE BOOTIES

Delivery guys are loath to take their shoes off. When they ring the bell, I present them with booties to save my clients' freshly laid floors and newly unfurled rugs.

26. SPACKLING KNIFE

After applying the Ready Patch, you have to use something to scrape off the excess. In a pinch, I have tried other things: a kitchen knife, a piece of cardboard, and a damp paper towel. Nothing else does the job like a spackling knife. Get one for less than $5, and keep it at your side.

27. WINDEX WIPES

Fingerprints get on the glass when framing a photo. Streaks show on the top of an acrylic coffee table after it's been moved. Why carry a whole bottle of Windex when I can just take a small pack of wipes?

28. WOOD MARKERS

Furniture that is less-than-perfect can sometimes get a new lease on life by coloring in its scratches with the correct color of wood marker. I suggest a set with several different shades, including black and white.

NAUGHTY WORD DICTIONARY

Don't use these words in my presence or in your designs.

ACCENT WALL

Painting or putting wallpaper on only one wall in a room screams cop-out. You wanted to go bold but were afraid to do it on all the walls. Go big or don't do it at all. See my two exceptions to this rule on page 100.

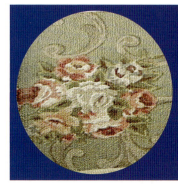

CHINTZ

As Great-Aunt Edna's calico curtains can attest, shiny cotton fabrics emblazoned with cabbage roses are much too much.

CHERRY

Red-toned woods are dated. Come to think of it, honey-toned woods are also passé.

CHRISTMAS LIGHTS

Once Christmas is over, these need to come down. Set a festive mood with candles or lamps with plug-in dimmers instead.

CLIP RINGS

Your college dorm called. It wants its drapery hardware back. Take the bed sheet window treatments down while you're at it.

COLLECTION

The minute friends/family hear that you are starting a collection, new additions start rolling in. Collections grow from interesting assortments to unruly junk piles in the blink of an eye.

CORDS

Electrical cords are the bane of my existence. We put a man on the moon, invented the Internet, and made fat-free potato chips. Why oh why can't we eliminate cords? Since (as of the publishing of this book) we can't, please do your best to conceal these eyesores.

CUSTOM

Custom costs too much and involves long lead times. Try and make retail work first. Custom is a last resort.

DECAL

These wanna-be murals can be practical in a nursery or playroom. But in adult spaces, any sort of decal is a definite don't.

DECORATIVE FINIAL

Keep the curtain rod's end caps basic so they don't steal the show from the drapery.

FAKE FIREPLACE

A fireplace is an architectural feature. If it's not built-in, it doesn't belong.

FAKE PLANT

From plastic ivy to overly-abloom orchids, fake plants are offenders. The other day a dear client emailed me to boast that she had bought the most beautiful silk arrangements for her office. I had to reply honestly: attractive fake flowers are an oxymoron.

FAKE ANYTHING

From fake art to fake Venetian plaster to fake hardwood flooring to fake stone, I can't think of anything that starts with the word fake that is stylish. Nope. Not one thing. It all looks like you wanted to get the real thing but cheaped out.

FAUX ANYTHING

See above, but this time read it with a French accent.

FLASH SALE SITE

Don't get stuck with impulse buys you can't return.

FURNITURE SET

Never buy a bedroom set, dining set, accent table set. Furniture pieces should GO together but never COME together. Shop a different store for a bed than its night-stands, a different store for a table than its chairs.

LOVESEAT

A pair of interesting side chairs is infinitely more interesting than this clunky sofa mini-me.

MATCHING

See Furniture Set

MICROFIBER

This unnatural fiber may scrub down easily, but that's its only attribute. It isn't breathable (lying on it or watch a movie or to take a nap will leave you sticky and sweaty). It is plagued with static issues, causing everything from crumbs to pet hair to cling. There are other types of performance fabrics that look less cheap.

PLEATHER

There's affordable and then there's atrocious.

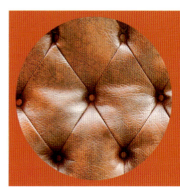

POPCORN CEILING
Same with the hair on your upper lip: Now that we have the technology to remove it, you should.

REUPHOLSTERY
Unless the piece is a priceless heirloom, it is more affordable and less of a hassle to buy a new sofa or chair than to recover it.

ROLLED ARM
Bulky arms on a chair or sofa take up valuable room space while lessening the seating surface area.

SHAG
Do you have a maid five days a week? Do you want a pet but don't have the time to walk one? Shag rugs are for you. Between the shedding and the entrapment of everything from stray hairs to Cheerios, this plush texture is high-maintenance and a breeding ground for peculiar particles.

SHEERS

Granny panties for your windows. Blousy, ill fitting, and blah, go for a blind instead.

SLIPCOVER

Granny panties for your upholstered furniture. I'd rather see a stained sofa than a saggy-baggy and wrinkled one.

SPONGE PAINT

We all know this one by now. No need to explain.

TABLE LINENS

A colleague of mine at Thom Filicia once told me that, other than napkins, all table linens (tablecloths, runners, placemats) are tacky and definitely not high-end. I am open to debate on this one. But ever since her comment, I can't look at them the same way.

TENSION ROD

Outside of a shower curtain, no other curtains should ever be hung on a tension rod. Not ever.

TOILET MAGAZINE RACK

Not only are these holders less than classy, their proximity to your flush means that the mags are covered in germy toilet water. Ack!

VALANCE

These bulbous, balloon-like treatments hang atop windows like hair-sprayed bangs from the '80s. Not only are they a trend that's past its time, they also cut off your window and its natural light.

WALL-TO-WALL CARPETING

My first thought when stepping onto or playing on top of wall-to-wall is, "What is trapped in here?" Unless it's brand new it never feels clean—and probably isn't. Renters get a pass. But buyers beware: This allergen-attracting synthetic floor treatment is not your friend.

WALLPAPER BORDER

No grapevines around a kitchen. No trains encircling a boy's room. No Laura Ashley floral following the ceiling-line of a bathroom. I was guilty of the latter in the late '90s, but now I know better. And now you do, too.

WORD ART

Love. Family. Believe. Create. Nauseate. Touchy-feely words hung or painted on walls do anything but inspire me. Don't tell me what to feel. Show me. Put up a pictorial piece that elicits an emotion without demanding it.

AUTHOR ACKNOWLEDGMENTS

As a business owner and mother of two toddlers, it took a supportive group of people to make this book happen. Firstly, I need to thank my agent, Christina Daigneault, who gave me the idea to write a book and found a way to make it a reality. I also want to thank my editor, Kristin Kulsavage, for her enthusiasm, accessibility, and assistance with translating my ideas to these pages. Much appreciation to Lallie Harling and her team for their help with the mood board images. Thanks to my photographer, John Ha, for his beautiful work.

Thank you to my family, my husband (Jack), babies (Jack and Eden), and dog (Carson), who went long stretches without their wife/mama so I could work on my book baby. Thank you to our nanny, Cherise Fletcher, who picked up the childcare and housekeeping slack. I am very appreciative for the keen editing eyes of my mother (Donna Head) and my mother-in-law (Janet Helmuth). Thanks always to my extended family, the MacKenzies and the Akers, for their support.

Gratitude goes out to my hardworking Affordable Interior Design team: the talented designers, Kelsey Surock and Rachel Madden. Special acknowledgment to Kelsey for helping to create and implement the design concepts on pages 23, 32, and 47. Thanks to my dedicated handymen, Ed DeJesus, Neil Christopherson, Orlando Garcia, and Marek Lachut, who lifted, assembled, and hung the pieces in these interior shots.

Big *bisous* to the Bataillon family for letting me smear their design magazines with Nutella. I was introduced to interior design at their breakfast table. During my high school summer breaks, I was an exchange student in the south of France and was practically adopted as a member of their family. Every morning, I would wake up early so I could eat a baguette while it was still warm from the bakery. With all five of my "sisters" asleep, the only thing to do while I ate was read Mrs. Bataillon's stacks of design magazines. I went through them as voraciously as I did the bread/tubs of hazelnut spread.

When I was at Thom Filicia, another apprentice there became my first design mentor. Katie Burke and I would go out for beer, and I would pick her brain, begging her to tell me everything she learned in design school. Her help and guidance gave me the confidence to take my first solo clients. I still use the rules she shared with me, and I put quite a few in this book.

I need to thank the cafes of Park Slope. Hemingway had Paris's LaCoupole; Kerouac had Manhattan's Café Reggio; I had the welcoming ambiance of Brooklyn coffee shops in which I wrote this book. Thanks to the kind staff and accessible electrical outlets at Tea Lounge (specifically Ian and Rex), Du Jour Bakery (whose delicious brioche I credit with the seven pounds I gained during the book's creation), Kos Kaffe (specifically Mike and Oliver), and the gang at Postmark Café.

I am very grateful to the clients who let me back into their homes to shoot pictures for this book. Most especially, a shout-out to Keri Svancara whose lovely space has practically been deemed the official apartment of Affordable Interior Design.

Finally, a big thanks to all my clients, design students, and readers. To me, there is nothing better than living within your means while also living in the home of your dreams. It is my sincere hope that my tips unlock and inspire your inner designer.

PHOTOGRAPHER ACKNOWLEDGMENTS

Thanks so much to Betsy for making this wonderful book happen for us. I love your drive and enthusiasm!

Thanks to Christina Daigneault for her grace, wit, and support.

And thank you to my wonderful wife, Bethany, for supporting me in all of my adventures.

PHOTOGRAPHY CREDITS